FURNITURE for the WORKPLACE

FURNITURE for the WORKPLACE

Linda Foa

Architecture & Interior Design Library

An Imprint of

PBC INTERNATIONAL, INC.

Distributor to the book trade in the United States and Canada:

Rizzoli International Publications Inc.
300 Park Avenue South
New York, NY 10010

Distributor to the art trade in the United States and Canada:

PBC International, Inc.
One School Street
Glen Cove, NY 11542
1-800-527-2826
Fax 516-676-2738

Distributed exclusively in India by:

Super Book House
Sind Chambers, Shahid Bhagat Singh
Road, Colaba, Bombay-400 005

Distributor throughout the rest of the world:

Hearst Books International
1350 Avenue of the Americas
New York, NY 10019

Library of Congress Cataloging-in-Publication Data

Foa, Linda, 1942-
    Furniture for the workplace   /   by Linda Foa.
            p.   cm.
    Includes index.
    ISBN 0-86636-175-8
    1. Office furniture industry--United States--Directories.
    2. Office furniture--Catalogs.   3. Office furniture--Standards--
    United States.   I. Title.
    HD9803.U62F63   1992
    684.1'0029'473--dc20
                                        92-2945
                                        CIP

CAVEAT—Information in this text is believed accurate, and will pose
no problem for the student or casual reader. However, the author was
often constrained by information contained in signed release forms,
information that could have been in error or not included at all. Any
misinformation (or lack of information) is the result of failure in these
attestations. The author has done whatever is possible to insure
accuracy.

Color separation, printing and binding by
Toppan Printing Co. (H.K.) Ltd. Hong Kong

Typography by
TypeLink, Inc.

Printed in Hong Kong

10 9 8 7 6 5 4 3 2 1

To the "comfort factors" in my environment
my husband
Conrad Foa
and our sons
Justin & Barrett

CONTENTS

FOREWORD

You'd think nothing could be more modern than today's office environment. Just glance at all the computers and their electronic accessories, orthopedically correct or "ergonomic" seating, and futuristic looking work surfaces and storage units. But look more closely at the details.

Why is an executive's office so large, empty and frequently unoccupied, whereas a clerk's space is so small it overflows with office machines, paper and personal effects? Why are the chairs with the most sophisticated controls reserved for managers, who may get in and out of them at will, while those for operational workers, confined to their workstations tending computers, papers and telephones, have so few adjustments to increase their sitters' comfort? Why are there personal electric fans, space heaters, desk lamps and portable radios scattered throughout offices supposedly equipped with the latest in air handling systems, task/ambient lighting fixtures and acoustical ceilings? Why has office productivity failed to show significant gains despite all the state-of-the-art computers and office furnishings lavished on office workers?

The truth is, many of today's offices still bear the marks of their lineage from turn-of-the-century forebears. When architect Peter Ellis designed the Oriel Chambers in Liverpool in 1864, he created a long, narrow, four-story structure of small, repetitive suites of rooms for two to three persons lining both sides of a hallway that ran the full length of the building. Each suite resembled a residential apartment, which suited its tenants just fine. By 1894, architect Louis Sullivan had conceived a 12-story skyscraper in Buffalo, the Guaranty Building, that simply repeated the pattern in a U-shape, stacked higher and deeper thanks to the invention of the elevator and electric (incandescent) light.

Five years later, architect Frank Lloyd Wright would break the mold in Buffalo with the Larkin Building, an airy, spacious environment in which desks stretched in rows towards the horizon beneath a four-story atrium. Then, despite the appearance of fluorescent light, central heating and air conditioning, acoustical suspended ceilings, and movable, demountable partitions, the form of the office stopped evolving and froze—for decades. Whether an organization preferred totally open spaces of "bullpens," neat, factory-like grids of desks and chairs, or rabbit warrens of private offices, where size might symbolically vary with the status of the occupant, or some combination of the two would be of little consequence to the developers of new office buildings in the years leading up to and immediately following World War II. The die had been cast, and the office furniture that prevailed since the turn of the century, including the desk, the credenza, the table and a host of office chairs of varying degrees of discomfort, accompanied the white-collar work force like a faithful dog.

Wonderful commercial architecture was born of this period, to be sure. Cass Gilbert's Woolworth Building in New York of 1913,

Reinhard & Hofmeister, Corbett, Harrison & MacMurray, and Hood & Fouilhoux's Rockefeller Center in New York of 1932, Frank Lloyd Wright's S.C. Johnson & Company in Racine, Wisconsin of 1936, and Skidmore, Owings & Merrill's Lever House in New York of 1952 are but a handful of the noble landmarks a rapidly industrializing United States would erect on its coasts and plains. Yet the agent of change in the office would have to come from within these great edifices. Business leaders—not architects or real estate developers—would have to change the way they conducted their office operations to change the form of the office.

It would be hard to say exactly what triggered the reconfiguration of the bullpen and the rabbit warren. After all, advances in building technology tend to trail breakthroughs in information processing, transportation and the global economy. So architecture, engineering and interior design can take credit at the most for playing midwife to the revolution that produced the partly open, partly enclosed work environment known as the open-plan office.

As has happened before in America's history, one key agent of change came from abroad. When the Quickborner Team of management consultants brought the concept of office landscaping or *bürolandschaft* from Germany to the United States in the 1960s, its impact was sudden and spectacular. You had only to visit the office of DuPont's Freon Division in Wilmington in 1967 to realize that a new age of white-collar work was proclaiming its arrival. Gone were walls, doors and private offices. Instead, furniture and freestanding screens were arranged to mirror circular communication patterns or "bubble diagrams" rather than orthogonal circulation grids.

Why did *bürolandschaft* fail both in Europe and the United States? Living with the freeform concept required too much discipline and effort simply to find your way through the maze or to perform your daily tasks without distracting or being distracted by your colleagues nearby. Yet it spurred on research that had already been underway here by proclaiming that the modern office could be planned to reflect patterns of activity rather than organizational hierarchy.

In effect, *bürolandschaft* implied that if what you *did* were more important than who you *were*, offices and office furniture should be chosen to suit your task and not your title. Standard furniture, such as a 36-inch by 60-inch desk with a 40-inch return, could easily serve the typical American secretary before the postwar years because office clerical work was largely routine and highly regimented. After the Baby Boomers began flooding the white-collar work force in the late 1960s with college-educated managers and professionals, however, what one employee did could differ dramatically from the next.

Creating custom office furniture for the Boomers using traditional methods was out of the question, of course. Not only would the cost be prohibitive, but the furniture risked being so specific to time and place that it might be rendered obsolete overnight. In fact, starting in the 1970s and spanning the 1980s, corporate America did go under the financial knife with a passion to restructure, decentralize, merge, acquire or gorge itself on debt through massive leveraged buy-outs.

No less important was the introduction of the personal computer in 1981, releasing awesome data processing power from the office "computer room" and scattering it across the general office floor, trailing miles of wiring. Obviously, traditional office furniture had never been designed to handle anything like this. Business leaders did not need rocket scientists to see that each new generation of computers and other electronic devices, unlike the telephone, the typewriter and the adding machine, would continuously bump its predecessor out of the office—and overrun standard desks and credenzas in the process.

At this moment, the work of two gifted Americans, architect and industrial designer George Nelson and artist and industrial designer Robert Propst, took center stage in the drama. Nelson had developed various prototype home modular storage systems in the 1940s that home owners could purchase as components, adding more units as the need arose. When he was joined by Propst in the 1950s at Herman Miller, Inc., a manufacturer of residential and commercial furniture at the time, the two proceeded to develop the idea of furniture as a "kit of parts" for office use. One of the most memorable results of their lengthy collaboration was "Action Office," which made its debut in 1963, as an elegant ensemble of freestanding and wall-hung office furniture and furniture components.

"Action Office" was so superbly crafted in its initial version that it proved too costly for the mass market. However, by 1968, Propst had perfected a new "Action Office" that represented a complete rethinking of office furniture. Instead of placing office workers and their furniture in private offices or bull-pens, Propst built partially enclosed offices around them using separate work surfaces and storage units suspended on cantilevered arms from vertical panels of varying heights that stopped short of the ceiling. Like *bürolandschaft*, there were no walls, doors or private offices in the new "open-plan" office. Whereas traditional furniture was placed *in* space, Propst's kit of parts or "furniture system" defined space by its own presence—it *was* the space.

With the arrival and swift acceptance of furniture systems and the "open-plan office" they created came many related innovations. Lighting products were designed to illuminate the open-plan office by distributing indirect light using "ambient" fixtures and focusing direct light with "task" fixtures. Wiring was routed horizontally over the floor inside raceways hidden in the vertical panels or tucked into the ceilings, floors or raised floors. Accessories were created to attach to and work with the furniture system in order to hold papers, telephones, office supplies

and the like. Orthopedically correct or "ergonomic" seating, a concept that emerged in the 1920s with Pipp's Pep Chair of 1921, Gunlocke's Washington Chair of 1923 and Harter's Executive Posture Chair of 1927, was revived by a crop of talented, young industrial designers eager to reinterpret ergonomic theory with fresh ideas and materials.

Every revolution must suffer the indignity of aging, and the open-plan office was no exception. Signs of its own mortality had begun to show as its role as a universal office revealed hidden flaws. As promised, it enabled each office worker to customize his or her workstation for the specific task at hand, frequently using less space per person than before—a genuine plus in a time of soaring real estate prices. It also lent itself to reconfiguration by being an assemblage of parts, business equipment that could be depreciated the way traditional office walls and doors could not.

Yet the white-collar organization was changing once more. From the close of the 1980s to the present, numerous developments have been forcing the hands of corporate and institutional leaders: the deepening integration of personal computers, local area networks, facsimile machines and printers with all aspects of office work; the catastrophic impact of excessive financial leverage, real estate speculation and global competition on American businesses; the down-sizing of the corporation through dismissals of entire layers of management and streamlining of operations; and the empowerment of teams of line personnel to make strategic decisions

on their own. Contemporary office furniture—relatively static despite claims that today's workstations are easy to assemble and disassemble, exposed to a fault in the view of workers longing to regain some measure of privacy, and increasingly implicated in reports of occupational disorders and injuries stemming from the use of computers and other office machines—may be entangled in as many new problems as it solved some two decades ago.

On the doorstep of another millennium, the modern IBM, AT&T or GM finds itself needing mobility to form project teams and to support them for as long as they are useful, within the framework of a much leaner management structure of semi-autonomous units. Furniture to satisfy this *modus operandi* may have to be light, nimble and versatile in form and function. In addition, it will probably be required to promote the health of office workers by positively affecting their posture, vision, breathing and hearing—at the same time it provides them the business tools they must use to work, and a visual environment that makes sense of their efforts.

Have we truly left the Oriel Chambers of 1864 behind us? Yes and no. Given the tremendous information processing power that the personal computer now places in the hands of the individual, tomorrow's great force for change in the global economy may be flashing on the computer screen at this very moment in somebody's home office.

Roger Yee
Editor-in-Chief
Contract Design

PREFACE

Furniture for the Workplace is a compendium of the most significant, functional and well-designed contract furnishings available on the market today. The book is presented as an information resource, providing a selection of some 200 products in seven important categories. Although design excellence was a primary criterion in the selection process, Furniture for the Workplace is not about architectural statement furniture. Rather, it is about functional furniture that means business, with emphasis on products that speak to VDT requirements as spelled out by the American National Standards Institute/Human Factors Society (ANSI/HFS) and other workplace-related standards.

Furniture that offers flexibility, adjustability and provision for the increasing demands of the electronic office determines the specification parameters of the 1990s, continuing the trend set in the 1980s. However, the dynamics of events have dimmed the expectations of unbridled growth and expansion promised by the boom economy of that gilded decade.

The subtext of Furniture for the Workplace reflects the responsible reaction of manufacturers to the challenges posed by these unpredicted events. The products shown in these pages satisfy the realities of a depressed market while meeting the stringent guidelines and legislation relating to workplace adjustability, flammability codes, and the provisions of the Americans with Disabilities Act.

Innovative strategies that override the negative effects of the office furniture surplus due to the mergers, acquisitions and resulting corporate restructuring of recent years include:

- Add-on elements that upgrade existing furniture to attain higher levels of efficiency and productivity.

- Freestanding components that expand the usefulness of new systems and integrate with existing systems, adding to the flexibility of workstation configuration in accommodating a variety of tasks in the changing office environment.

- Finishes in a wider choice of materials and colors that reduce the cost implications of tighter client budgets as well as more prudent long-term facility investment management and planning.

- Commitment to product testing that assures compliance with ANSI/HFS and other health-related standards.

- Continued research and development that addresses the issues of the electronic workplace and the reduction of task-related stress and injuries.

- Greater awareness that technology is the tool of human ingenuity and not its master.

Furniture for the Workplace shows that, for the contract industry, the 1990s may well be the most stimulating and rewarding decade in a century of extraordinary progress that began with Frank Lloyd Wright's landmark Larkin Building, where the planned office environment had its genesis. Today the competitive edge has never been sharper, and the need for proactive attitudes never more clearly indicated.

On the cusp of a new century, there is evidence in these pages that the cooler economy offers a necessary window of opportunity to set a new course toward establishing the foundation of a healthier and more productive workplace in the third millennium. Furniture for the Workplace provides a reference map that shows how far the industry has reached to attain that goal.

Linda Foa

CHAPTER ONE

FURNITURE SYSTEMS

Panel-based, Freestanding, Desking

In the decade of the 1990s, sociological, economic and technological factors have come to play dominant roles in facility management and design. There are, for example, increasing numbers of women with managerial and administrative responsibilities who require a change of scale in furniture, and prefer a more personal ambiance in the executive office. As the computer literate "baby boom" generation advances to executive status, computer technology must be accommodated at ever higher levels of the corporate hierarchy. Technology also impacts the young "baby bust" generation of the 1970s now entering the work force. This group places high quality-of-life expectations and demands on the office environment: clean air, acoustical control, and amenities such as exercise facilities and flex time. Corporate restructuring and realignment results in a more democratic culture in the work-

place. And, as the private office moves onto the endangered species list, project team management becomes the style of many corporations and institutions. Paradoxically, the need for privacy becomes more intense. "Privacy," however, is defined more in terms of protecting sensitive and confidential documents and conversations, than in the egos of higher management.

These factors significantly impact the thinking of manufacturers as they address the realities of the contemporary marketplace. Furniture systems are here to stay. However, as the workplace continues to evolve, reflecting change in the styles and processes of office work itself, the application of systems to the office environment becomes more complex: a one-size-fits-all approach no longer suffices to satisfy end-user needs.

Four distinct workplace models appeared in the course of the office evolution from the 1950s until the end of the 1980s. Each one, in its time, was seen as the solution to every problem of efficiency and productivity. Today's experts now recommend integrating aspects of all four models to achieve optimum results in this decade and beyond.

Enclosed Offices are most appropriate for professionals such as lawyers and accountants who require four walls and a ceiling to ensure control over extraneous noise and distracting activities, as well as security of confidential documents. As computer literacy becomes more extensive among these professionals and executives, their need for more functional and adaptable furnishings is expected to increase dramatically.

Bullpen Offices are suitable for people who perform repetitive tasks and who have no need for visual or acoustical privacy. Other advantages of the bullpen include easy interaction among co-workers on project team assignments. The ability to reconfigure bullpen components to meet changed requirements is a further benefit of this relatively inexpensive model.

Uniform Open Plan refines the bullpen principle, allowing increasing levels of privacy, and by virtue of panel-based partition components, provides the storage and electronic support needed for computer-related tasks. The uniform plan is both space-efficient and cost-effective.

Free-Form Open Plan is the most recently developed model, incorporating many of the features of the Uniform Open Plan. Driven by the "project team management" concept, the Free-Form Open Plan uses either free-standing or wall-hung surfaces, storage and other components, affording an appropriate amount of visual/acoustical privacy, as well as cabling and wiring for advanced computer technology and telecommunications. Each workstation module is expressly designed to support the specific needs of individual team members. Groups of six or more workstations can be configured to reflect the interactive requirements of an entire team.

Finally, furniture systems used in any or all of the models described, incorporate the flexibility necessary to accommodate the sophisticated technology and work styles of the emerging global economy. "Flexibility" continues to be a primary requirement, as does price sensitivity. The systems shown here offer different combinations of function, design and price that best satisfy the needs of specifiers and users.

AURORA support staff workstations.

AURORA transaction counter between workstations.

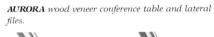

AURORA wood veneer conference table and lateral files.

AURORA workstations with distinctive rounded radii detailing and colorful accent stripe.

Syntrax II

Syntrax II is a linking desk system with ergonomic features based on the original Syntrax system, designed by Bob Worrell in 1988. Introduced in 1992, Syntrax II is a freestanding system with linking work surfaces, accessory consoles, and privacy screens. The system's desking units can be connected in a straight line, or in two-, three- and four-way configurations for unlimited task and application solutions. Three levels of storage options can be added to fit any application—overhead cabinets and shelves, work surface consoles, office management accessories and pedestal storage. The unique design of the high- and low-profile consoles provides visual privacy while maintaining air circulation and ventilation essential in electronic intensive environments. An accessory console with built-in channels runs the length of the work surface. The channels accommodate a variety of items such as paper trays, a telephone tray, and a light bracket, all of which can be strategically placed on the console. The console tackboard offers an element of color and texture. An articulating keyboard arm pulls out from under the work surface, and a processing unit with a disk drive for a personal computer can also be stored there. Simple electrical and data wire management is integral to the system. Syntrax II is a steel furniture system available in a wide range of standard paint finishes with laminate work surfaces in standard colors. The consoles come in a variety of fabrics with a selection of panel trim colors.

Syntrax II linking desk system with accessory consoles and privacy screens.

AMERICAN SEATING COMPANY

American Seating Company is a privately held company headquartered in Grand Rapids, Michigan.

Framework,™ Framework Clusters, Invitation™ Wood

Introduced in 1978, American Seating System was renamed System R in 1982 and Framework in 1990. The system is panel-based with panel-hung components including work surfaces, overheads, storage pedestals, and lighting. Rugged steel frames with removable panel inserts can be changed without tools to replace fabric or to interchange it with steel, glass, or wood. Modifications in 1982 included revising the system's electric power capabilities and updating the styling.

In 1985, System R's horizons were extended to accommodate different professional activities and environments. It is one of the only systems where varied environments can be built off the same framework, for example, panels can form a double panel chase to provide routing for laboratory utilities.

The system offers a full line of task-specific components and accessories such as integrated casework cabinetry, drawers, sinks and lab grade laminate tops.

The Invitation™ Wood collection, now part of Framework, was introduced in 1988. Geared to executives, the system also offers matching wood trim for support staff workstations. The warm wood tones soften the ambiance of the workplace. Components include work surfaces and overhead storage, as well as freestanding tables.

Framework continues to emphasize the concept that the framework of one furniture system can accommodate the different environments of the office, laboratory, technical assembly, and health care workstations. An integrated furniture system for business or institution, it offers increased power and wire capacity, softened work surface edges and corners, and curvilinear shapes. The streamlined components feature radius edge details. Heavy-duty steel frames and removable panel inserts form the core of one system that can accommodate radically different work environments.

Framework Clusters offer a comprehensive portfolio of panel heights and widths and a broad selection of work surface sizes and shapes to provide clover, curvilinear, serpentine, or hexagonal-shaped configurations. Each Framework Cluster may be planned as a freestanding unit or linked with adjacent clusters to form a larger unit.

Framework *workstations for (left to right) office, health care, lab, and technical assembly work environments.*

Framework workstations with pass-through panel and overhead storage.

Framework's curvilinear work surfaces offer "within arm's reach" ergonomic benefits.

Framework Invitation Wood with Integrated Table System.

THE GUNLOCKE COMPANY

The Gunlocke Company is a division of HON Industries and is headquartered in Wayland, New York.

Prism System

In 1978 Heibert introduced the IPA System and in 1986 expanded, refined and renamed it the Prism System. In 1989 HON Industries acquired The Gunlocke Company, closed its Heibert Carson, California, plant, and moved the Prism product line to Gunlocke's wood manufacturing facility in Wayland, New York. Prism's steel components are made in Corry, Pennsylvania, by CorryHeibert. The Prism System offers both panel-supported components for clustered open-plan workstations, and freestanding casegoods for the private office. Prism's wide range of standard components features a broad offering of materials and design detail options, thereby encouraging diversity and customization.

Overheads and storage pedestals are available as all wood, polyurethane painted medium density fiberboard, all steel, or any combination thereof. The line ranges in materials and price from hand-crafted cabinetry and wood surfaces to metal files and plastic laminates. Standard materials include 5 premium veneers, 20 wood finishes, and 12 opaque paint finishes and matching plastic laminates. Panels are available factory- or field-electrified with a 7-wire system that provides for 3 circuits including a dedicated/isolated ground circuit. Work surfaces are available in wood veneers with solid wood edging, laminate, and laminate with wood edges. Four top configurations include standard and P-shaped conference ends. Four edge profiles include plain, radiused, and mitered. Freestanding pieces such as cabinets, closets, storage units, and bookcases are offered in matching edge profiles.

Prism's *options range from hand-crafted cabinetry to economical metal components with wood laminate work surfaces.*

Prism's *executive office in one of five premium wood veneers.*

Haworth, Inc.

Haworth, Inc. is a leading multinational manufacturer of furniture and furniture systems. It is a privately held company located in Holland, Michigan.

UniGroup

UniGroup was the first office system to offer panel-integrated electrical power when it was introduced in 1976. Today it offers two electrical systems: TriCircuit introduced in 1978, and Power Base™ introduced in 1986. The latter is an 8-wire system that provides multiple dedicated circuits, separate neutrals, and access to an isolated ground wire.

UniGroup is comprised of basic components such as work surfaces, overhead cabinets, storage pedestals, and paper management accessories. The panel-based system features rectilinear and curved panels with fabric-covered and/or glazed inserts. Component materials are metal or wood construction with laminate or wood veneer surfaces. The system also features task lights under overhead cabinets, and panel-suspended ambient lighting. Work surfaces are available in a choice of four edge treatments with wood or laminate tops. Storage cabinets are available with laminate, fabric or wood surface treatments.

UniGroup pass-through panels allow two workers to share the same terminal without sacrificing privacy.

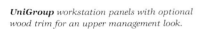

UniGroup workstation panels with optional wood trim for an upper management look.

23

UniGroup managerial station with conferencing area and multiple storage options.

UniGroup D-shaped convergents can be attached to any perpendicular work surface, or mounted directly to a panel.

UniGroup corner work surfaces feature an optional adjustable keyboard pad.

UniGroup Clusters

UniGroup Clusters, introduced in 1990, feature four unique work surface shapes which can be combined to form three-, four-, five- or six-station clusters. Cluster work surfaces work in conjunction with the standard UniGroup panels, components and accessories. Work surfaces have a curved front edge and can accommodate interaction and conferencing. The 120-degree planning angles maximize usable work surface and aisle space, yet provide ample room for visitors. A minimum number of parts simplifies installation and inventory planning.

UniGroup Clusters workstation configurations can be created by simply adding or deleting work surfaces and panels; a five-station cluster is easily converted to six.

UniGroup Clusters feature wide-angle contoured surfaces.

PLACES

Haworth introduced PLACES in 1988 as an upgrade to UniGroup. Virtually a second generation panel system to the original UniGroup, PLACES offers improved aesthetics and performance including wire management upgrades such as: top raceways for laying in communication cables; and ported panels for access to power and communications cabling at the work surface. It also offers more refined panel connections for better alignment and a cleaner look. The system components include: work surfaces, flipper door overhead cabinets, and suspended and freestanding pedestals. Components can be specified in freestanding and panel-mounted configurations, and are available in a vast collection of laminates, matching paint colored metals, and/or rich wood veneers. PLACES is the platform for several developments including two freestanding and panel-integrated casegood lines in steel and wood, as well as a complementary lateral file and storage system. The extensive casegood lines feature: lateral files, storage pedestals, vertical storage units, credenzas, wardrobe/storage units, desks and returns, and D-shaped convergent work surfaces.

PLACES elements provide a common design statement enabling freestanding and panel-mounted configurations to be integrated.

PLACES fixed pedestals and credenza files are designed to support work surfaces.

PLACES convergent table creates a focus for interactions, while transition and corner elements make the most of valuable space.

Architectural Elements

The panel shapes for Architectural Elements were developed in 1989 to provide a means for creating interior architecture and to expand the design possibilities of PLACES. Architectural Elements consists of geometric glazed and fabric-covered panels, fanlights, and single and double (French) doors that not only give personality to the workplace, but provide a unique visual perspective to those in it. The elements bring a neighborhood cityscape feeling to corporate spaces because each department can take on a distinctive, more individualized approach. The hierarchy of an office can be addressed by the creation of "landmarks" throughout the space. Architectural Elements is compatible with PLACES and UniGroup systems furniture.

Architectural Elements workstations with glazed door and fanlight.

Architectural Elements glazed panels provide transparency in an office environment.

New Views

Haworth's New Views was designed in 1991 to offer a fresh viewpoint in office planning and to expand the flexibility of its PLACES system. New Views can add varying typography to the sea of panels and modular units so prevalent in offices. The items center around a versatile storage tower that can create landmarks or space definition in the office. The towers, available with swing or pocket doors, come in different heights and function as coat closets, bookcases, and storage pedestals.

The New Views products are designed to produce effective task team environments by providing: lower panel heights without sacrificing acoustical privacy; work surfaces in curvilinear shapes for easier transition between tasks; corner canopies for a sheltered workplace and acoustical privacy; flexible overhead lights that adjust to the task and environment; and panel alternatives with customized inserts for visual relief and for improved natural light and air circulation. Other available products are: additional communications and power outlet options to support electronic communication; pieces to satisfy conferencing needs; and tools that help organize the individual and provide task flexibility.

New Views offers specifiers the ability to create both private and social areas within the same workspace, to support multiple tasks within a workstation, and to provide for more personal organization.

New Views work areas with flexible overhead lights.

New Views task team environment.

New Views corner workspace with over-head can-
opy and curvilnear work surface.

New Views storage towers.

RACE

RACE offers a winning combination of two distinct groups of office systems—flexible freestanding office furniture along with such panel-system pluses as: visual and acoustical privacy, power and cable management advantages, and improved space utilization. The system, designed by Douglas Ball in 1978, is built around a horizontal beam at the work surface level which carries power and cabling, and helps organize the components. The system can be built-up from the beam to create seated or standing privacy by adding upper structure and privacy pads (tiles). Users can add on or move work surfaces, upper structures, storage, paper management, and lighting anywhere on the beam or upper structure to suit individual needs. Privacy pads can be added incrementally to create varying degrees of openness or enclosure and to permit the flow of air and light.

Since Haworth added RACE to its stable of systems, design enhancements have been made to allow the following: easier installation and access to wiring harnesses and cables; more receptacle locations for greater planning flexibility; increased lay-in capability for electrical wiring which allows fast, economical installation and reconfiguration; access ports that allow quick snap-in connections and accommodate modules for voice/data communication; and post trim interconnects at the raceway for a cleaner profile at ends and corners. In addition, Haworth has added new overhead storage units and a privacy screen that attaches to bullet-shaped work surfaces.

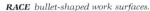

RACE bullet-shaped work surfaces.

RACE overhead storage units with built-up privacy tiles.

KINETICS
A Haworth Portfolio Company

Powerbeam and Powerbeam2

The Powerbeam desking system, introduced in 1983, was designed by Paulo Favaretto and James Hayward. It offers flexibility and affordable redesign in the workplace. The system's privacy panels suspend 12 inches below the work surface and rise to a choice of three different heights above it—13 inches for open viewing, 22 inches for visual privacy, and 32 inches to hold overhead storage units. Since its panels do not extend to the floor, the system gives an appearance of openness while offering greater air circulation. The freestanding and modular collection of executive, management and general office desks, credenzas, machine desks and returns can be set up, or taken down and rearranged, in a matter of hours. Top supporting bridges are clamped to the Powerbeam for easy installation and desk top changes.

The Powerbeam, supported by trestle bases, serves as the arterial passageway for the desk system. Inside, its two segregated channels house the electrical and communication cables that are fed through an added tube that runs down to the floor. Hinged doors provide access to each compartment. The series can be specified as individual units and/or used in conjunction with connector tops to form workstations with a minimum number of trestle base supports to the floor. The desks and modular desk components are available with or without factory-installed electrical elements.

Introduced in 1991, Powerbeam2 provides enhancement gable panels, designed by James Hayward, for added privacy and internal cable management of Powerbeam. The end panels en-

close the Powerbeam desk's open trestle base and provide a concealed wire feed by channeling it into the leg. The panel's tapered design permits pedestals to fit against the panel, yet provides access to pedestal drawers with side pulls.

Powerbeam and Powerbeam2 offer under-the-work-surface storage pedestals, end panels, beams and trestles in a choice of 31 Kinetics Kinkote painted epoxy colors. Work surfaces can be ordered in plastic laminate, hand-matched and laid-up wood veneers, or ¾-inch thick clear float glass with eased and polished edges. Accessory elements such as catalog holders, letter trays, and task lighting can be hung on the panels. Plastic clips allow the organizational elements to vertically stack one under the other. The two systems can easily mix to work together.

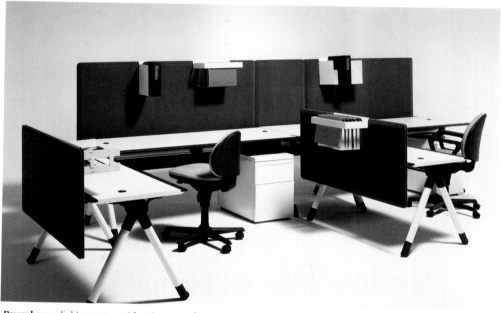

Powerbeam desking system with privacy panels.

Powerbeam2 trestle-based desking system.

PREMISE™

In response to a cost conscious marketplace, Haworth introduced PREMISE in 1992. The line is geared to offer a complete range of high-value office furniture designed to meet the needs of small-and medium-size businesses. Its scope extends from panel systems to freestanding desks, files, and bookcases, all of which are totally interchangeable. In an effort to simplify the office furniture specification, purchase, and installation process, Haworth's PREMISE offers: a comprehensive list of standard features, component flexibility, and the most frequently specified product options.

The 3-inch thick panels are the basic element of the PREMISE system. Constructed with a steel frame and honeycomb core, they combine a tackable surface with acoustical performance. Because of the panel's integrated alignment and hidden hardware, panel runs look like a wall rather than a furniture system. To ensure the need for privacy, PREMISE offers tall panels and a lockable door as well as windowed and lower-height panels for more interaction. Standard panels include: three circuits with one that is completely isolated to protect sensitive electronic equipment; triplex receptables to permit access to electrical power through as many as 12 outlets per panel; power and communication ports above or below the work surface; concealed cable management in top and base raceway plus two vertical channels; and the critical 6-inch radius requirements for glass fiber telephone cables.

Softly radiused work surfaces, available in laminate or wood veneer finishes, come in a variety of shapes for different tasks, such as corners for computers and D shapes for conferencing. PREMISE work surfaces can be hung on panels supported by storage components, and are height adjustable even when the surface is supported by a pedestal or file.

Storage alternatives include: overheads, lateral files, drawer pedestals, mobile pedestals, and storage cabinets. The full-front design of the units allows wood fronts to be used on steel cabinets for a quality look without the expense. Freestanding furniture includes: desks with concealed wireways, credenzas, files, bookcases, returns, bridges, and corners.

PREMISE office configuration in wood veneer finish.

PREMISE *workstation with corner computer units and D-shaped work surface for conferencing.*

PREMISE *workstation in metal and laminate.*

PREMISE *offers tall panels for privacy and lower-height panels for interaction.*

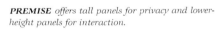

THE HON COMPANY

The HON Company is a manufacturer of moderately priced office furniture and furniture systems and is the largest division of HON INDUSTRIES, a publicly held company. Both are headquartered in Muscatine, Iowa. HON INDUSTRIES also owns CorryHiebert, BPI and The Gunlocke Company in Wayland, New York.

CONCENSYS®

CONCENSYS entered the marketplace in 1988. Its panel systems provide flexibility for open office planning with three design solutions: Systems, Modular, and Clusters. The solutions can work individually or in combination to create a network of work environments. The system panels are available with putty or light gray raceways and a selection of fabrics in over 100 colors. Work surfaces include peninsula tops and curvilinear corners, and are available in a selection of laminates from wood grain to solids in light gray or putty.

CONCENSYS features electric circuitry in upper and lower raceways. Optional vertical raceways bring power and communication cables from the top and bottom to work surface level for convenient plug-ins. Components include overhead storage cabinets and shelves, pedestals, and freestanding tables. The system is in the low to moderate price range.

CONCENSYS *executive workstation.*

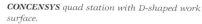

CONCENSYS *quad station with D-shaped work surface.*

CONCENSYS *quad station with pass-through panels.*

KIMBALL INTERNATIONAL, INC.

Kimball International, Inc.'s office furniture division includes Kimball Office Furniture Company and National Office Furniture Company. It is a multinational company that is publicly traded on the New York Stock Exchange and is headquartered in Jasper, Indiana.

Cetra®

Introduced in 1988, Cetra is a panel system with components that can work in open plan or private offices. System components include work surfaces, overhead cabinets, pedestals, and free-standing modular casegoods in a choice of solid woods, laminates, or metal. The casegoods can be fully integrated within the system environment or used to create freestanding configurations from desks and credenzas to L- and U-shaped units. Work surface choices include laminate, wood, and laminate with a wood rim or a resilient Durasoft edge.

Cetra features five panel heights to accommodate reception applications, privacy requirements, and employee interaction. Standard panels are tackable and acoustical with fabric on both sides, or wood/fabric combinations. Panel top and end caps are finished in stained or opaque wood for a quality look. Panels are available as either electrical or non-electrical, with power at the base and/or at the work surface. Curved panels can be specified in fabric, or wood/fabric combinations, as well as glazed in clear or smoke. Sectional panel frames accommodate tile inserts for windows and pass-throughs.

The Cetra system comes in a wide selection of solid woods including mahogany, walnut, oak, and maple in a variety of stains.

Cetra workstations in steel and laminate.

Cetra's varied panel heights accommodate both reception and office area applications.

Cetra workstation configuration with conference area.

Cetra workstations.

37

Footprint™

Footprint is a collection of components that offers functional, dimensional, and aesthetic interface between fixed-wall and open plan offices. It provides a bridge between panel-based systems and casegoods. Introduced in 1992, Footprint consists of three elements: TRAXX™ which are horizontal twin wall-mounted rails; modular storage components; modular work surface components and tiles. The various components allow optimum use of available space by adapting to the size and shape of the work space or building floor plan. Essentially, the system offers a panel look in offices without using panels. For open plan configurations, the Footprint TRAXX can be used in combination with Cetra panels.

The horizontal rails (tracks) are designed to suspend storage components, work surfaces, wall tiles, and accessories. Therefore, system components can be positioned anywhere along the perimeters of enclosed rooms, against walls or columns, and into corners. The components can also be configured as freestanding furniture. The unique aspect of TRAXX is that it eliminates the redundancy of systems panels in an enclosed office, and can provide a custom look with modular components.

Finish options include: a choice of three wood veneers—maple, mahogany and walnut in a selection of finishes: three standard laminates in haze, gray and black; and a choice of edge treatments on surfaces which are available in laminates of the customer's choice. A selection of fabrics and finishes is available for the wall tiles. Other tiles include acoustical fabric, wood and marker-board, and a slat tile for mounting file holders, varied size shelves, and work tools. Specifiers can also custom select their own laminates and fabrics for the system.

Footprint *Traxx horizontal rail system.*

Footprint *components suspended from Cetra panels.*

HARPERS
A subsidiary of Kimball International

Multiple Options

Multiple Options System was introduced by Harpers in 1984. It represents a comprehensive selection of panels and components, freestanding modular desks, returns and credenzas, electrical options, and filing and storage. All the units are designed to work together to create an efficient work environment.

Communication panels are standard tackable and acoustical with built-in raceways to provide separation of power and communications wiring. The panel offers three standard electrical systems: Power Option 1, 2 and 3. Multiple Options segmented panels are available in fabric, fabric and glazed, or open panel combinations. The system offers basic components such as work surfaces, receding door overheads, and pedestals. Continuous work surfaces are available in four standard shapes: rectangular, corner, adjoining, and piano. The tops can be specified in any size, dimension, and choice of materials in metal, laminate and wood. A line of freestanding furniture including desks, returns, and credenzas offers greater flexibility within the system. Work surface privacy and vertical storage can be achieved with the use of desk risers, whereas standing bookcases, lateral files, pedestals, and full-size media cabinets provide added storage.

Multiple Options freestanding modular desks and storage risers.

Multiple Options curvilinear configuration with wire management communications panels.

THE KNOLL GROUP

The Knoll Group is owned by the Westinghouse Electric Corporation, a multinational publicly owned company, headquartered in Pittsburgh, Pennsylvania. The Knoll Group is based in New York City.

Reff System 6

Reff System 6, introduced in 1982, is a premier wood office system with integrated technology support. Its quality and design simplicity are intended to appeal to executive and professional applications in traditional corporate environments. Although the system offers a limited number of parts and pieces, it is a full scope product. System 6 offers a range of double-cut and natural veneers as well as solid wood construction throughout its components which can be panel-hung or freestanding and include pedestal cases and drawers, overheads, and work surfaces. The Reff signature features dove-tail wood joinery, finished component backs, and a variety of detail

options. The line is entirely non-handed, with neither rights nor lefts, so it can easily be switched or flipped without any changes.

Reff System Z, introduced in 1988, is essentially the same as Reff System 6 but is available in a selection of laminate finishes to achieve a more reasonable price point. The system still maintains the design simplicity of System 6 but with the less expensive laminate finishes, and metal rather than wood interior drawer construction. Both systems have the Reff high performance acoustical panel with removable insets for ease of maintenance and reconfiguration.

Reff System 6

Morrison Network

Morrison Network delivers the integration of panel-based and sophisticated freestanding desk capabilities along with a wide range of components and finishes. The freestanding desk is the building block of Morrison Network's enhanced desking capabilities. Curvilinear work surfaces and the coordinating Knoll Interaction™ Tables are some of the design options. Vertical and kiosk storage units provide substantial capacity in a small footprint, whereas under-work-surface storage utilizes previously dead space. Power distribution and cable management are handled under the work surface. Grommets accommodate linked and back-to-back desks. Vertical cabling runs through desk legs and stanchion cavities. The system offers lots of flexibility and a broad scope of product finishes. Introduced in 1991, Morrison Network integrates thoroughly with the Morrison System, designed by Andrew Morrison and the Knoll Design and Development team in 1986.

The system's basic components consist of vertical panels, desk panels, work surfaces, and storage units, as well as task and fill lighting, and accessories. Materials range from laminates and metal to 6 hardwood veneers, 6 Techgrain™ wood veneers, and over 300 panel fabrics. Morrison was the first system to really hide its hardware to achieve the clean, architectural appearance so favored by designers. The system's unique recessed connector track serves double-duty by connecting and automatically leveling the vertical panels for perfect alignment. The connector track also includes a double-width slot that can be shared by two cantilevered components. Morrison offers four vertical panel heights to create a variety of spaces, from highly enclosed to completely open. Panel heights can easily be mixed. The system features either of its electrical systems in its base: the 3-circuit/6-wire, or the 4-circuit/8-wire 2 + 2™ Raceway which handles virtually any power distribution need, and provides two circuits for general-purpose electrical use and two for computer equipment so that sensitive information systems can be isolated.

In keeping with its concept of integrating new product into Morrison Network, The Knoll Group offers an overhead storage unit, with pneumatic spring door, and a curvilinear silhouette rather than the standard square shape. The unit can be hung on any size panel (for example, a 36-inch unit on a 30-inch panel). The trim exterior of the overhead unit offers maximum clearance for VDT monitors while its spacious interior features a unique system of dividers.

Morrison Network *freestanding desk.*

Morrison Network *office with Interaction Table and kiosk storage unit with optional cupola.*

Morrison Network curvilinear configuration for private or team office spaces.

Morrison Network work surfaces offer flexible planning.

Morrison Network freestanding privacy screen with storage kiosks.

Equity

Equity was initially introduced in 1984 as WesGroup/Equation by Westinghouse Furniture Systems which is now part of The Knoll Group. It is a panel-based system with a complete range of hanging components such as work surfaces, overheads, pedestals, lateral files, and work support accessories. A line of freestanding tables and desks is designed to interact with the system. The freestanding pieces are available in height-adjustable versions with optional adjustment controls including fully manual, spring-loaded counter force, or electronically power-assisted controls.

Equity's panel/post centerline modularity allows for predictable dimension measurement (from center of post to center of post even at T or 90-degree turns) and ease of layout configuration and reconfiguration. Since there is no creepage factor, additional workstations can be accommodated on each floor. The system's Equation enhancement panel provides technical support with data and communication capacity within the hinged raceway, vertically through connector tracks, and connected at panel tops. Top cap options add visual interest, and fabric covers added to the panel connections provide a monolithic appearance and easy access to the vertical raceway. Equity is a metal system which includes: overhead cabinets available in painted steel or fabric-covered fronts; storage pedestals in painted steel or injection molded plastic fronts; and work surfaces in laminated wood core or with a wood veneer option.

Equity workstations provide transaction counters for incoming work.

Equity management workstation features D-shaped tables for tasks and conferencing.

ExpanDesk/Tempo

ExpanDesk/Tempo was introduced in 1977 by Shaw Walker which is now owned by The Knoll Group. The system is an effective solution for task-intensive installations as well as more open teamwork plans. The combination of ExpanDesk's modular metal desking system and Tempo panels is an alternative to value-oriented, panel-based systems or conventional metal desks. The Tempo panel has acoustical ability and wiring capacity in its base and top raceways. The ExpanDesk furniture base offers full component modularity which includes desks, credenzas, and overdesk units in painted steel with material options such as laminate work surfaces and fabric wrapped overhead fronts. The system offers freestanding, panel-supported and integrated desk/panel solutions. It is especially appropriate for small businesses, government facilities, and operations-intensive offices.

ExpanDesk/Tempo combines ExpanDesk's modular metal desking system with Tempo panels.

HERMAN MILLER

Herman Miller is a leading multinational manufacturer of furniture and furniture systems. The Fortune 500, publicly held company has its headquarters in Zeeland, Michigan.

Action Office®

In 1964 a fundamental change in workplace design occurred with the introduction of the Action Office system. This revolutionary open plan concept evolved from several years of research, testing and design by Robert Propst and his staff at the Herman Miller Research Corporation in collaboration with George Nelson and Associates. Propst's thesis was generated by questions about the ways people actually work in offices. The answers resulted in a system of panels, work surfaces, and storage components that could be configured and reconfigured to support the individual work styles and processes of a particular person, department, or company.

Beginning with the addition of panels in 1968, Action Office has responded as the workplace itself changed, but the underlying concept remains constant. Propst's *The Office: A Facility Based on Change*, published in 1968, defined the systems criteria that have been maintained over the years, as lighting, electrical, and computer support components have been added to the original elements. Therefore, companies that installed the

first Action Office products almost 25 years ago, have had the ability to add to, update, and refurbish their office environments with minimal expense and disruption.

Propst's innovative solution was recognized in 1985 by the World Design Congress in Washington, D.C. as "The Best Design of the Past 24-years, 1961–1985." Action Office set the industry standards for the systems furniture that now pervades the contemporary workplace.

Action Office Series 2 Panels

By 1986, when Herman Miller introduced the Action Office Series 2 panels (originally called Action Office Encore), the workplace had absorbed the technological advances of the electronic era. At the same time, with acceptance of the Post-Modern aesthetic, developments in the office environment had "softened" the clean lines of modern furniture. Action Office Series 2 reflects the characteristics of the original system,

while responding to the demands of a more sophisticated workplace.

To meet the needs of this second generation, Action Office Series 2 panels with B-style components project a softened appearance, with rolled-edge cabinets, solid one-piece work surfaces, and finish options that include a choice of wood veneers. Personal work styles are enhanced with an accessory bar that supports a variety of work tools, which are designed to take supplies and paperwork off the work surface and help organize them. Increased electrical capacity for sensitive electronic equipment and baseline cable management features meet high-level industry standards.

Action Office Series 2 is designed to conform with the module and mechanical connections of the original Action Office system and the componentry of both is mutually compatible. As a result, long-term Action Office users can integrate the elements of Action Office Series 2 into the existing office landscape.

Action Office 2 with Series 2 panels and wood veneer peninsula table.

Action Office Series 2 multi-task office
environment.

Action Office Series 2 reception area with V-Wall
enclosed executive office.

Action Office Series 3 Panels

The evolution of Action Office system continued in 1991 with the introduction of Series 3 panels, intended for customers who need the highest level of panel-based energy and cable distribution. The panels include: top channel cable management; the separation of voice/data cables from electrical wires; and power and cable access at any height. They have a slim profile, with crisp panel step-downs, subtle connection detailing, and six top cap options. Series 3 panels were designed for Herman Miller by Virginia DuBrucq, a Denver, Colorado, interior architect, to accommodate the electronic equipment used in today's offices.

The features of Series 3 panels include: complete horizontal and vertical separation of power and cables; protection of data from electrical interference; power at both base and work surface height; fast and easy lay-in of power and cables; and compatibility with a wide range of components and freestanding furniture. The cable management panel is composed of a frame and removable face panels. Telecommunications cables are routed down from the top of the panel and electrical wires run upward from the base, meeting at the work surface.

The Action Office series panels are offered with two component options, A-style and B-style. A-style are the original Action Office components that continue to offer excellent performance capabilities and can be used with any panel produced since 1968. B-Style components provide refined edge details and more work surface options. They also can be used with any panel produced since 1968.

Action Office Series 3 panels offer power and cable access at any height.

Action Office Series 3 slim profile panels with maximum electrical capabilities.

Ethospace® Interiors

The principles of architecture inspire Ethospace Interiors, a furniture system designed by Bill Stumpf and a Herman Miller design team led by Jack Kelley in 1984. Its frame-and-tile structured walls provide freedom to vary horizons, textures, patterns and finishes. For example, glass and acoustical tiles can be positioned where needed, tiles can be pulled off for access to wiring, and damaged tiles can easily be replaced. Ethospace permits the blending of different types of offices including private or open, bullpen arrangements, or more expansive configurations. It represents intelligent office planning based on human scale, attention to personal work styles, and the need for intercommunication, as well as privacy within the office landscape.

Architectural detailing is combined with frame-and-tile construction, facilitating installation and functional and aesthetic change. Sturdy 3-inch "wall" frames can be clad with surface tiles in a variety of colors and materials. Transparent tiles create windows to perimeter and other natural light sources. Rail tiles support tools that organize work. Acoustical tiles absorb sound.

Ethospace consists of overhead cabinets, free-standing and suspended storage pedestals, rectangular and corner work surfaces, and the more dramatic round-end and rectangular peninsula work surfaces. Support cabinets, including work and coat cabinets with or without shelves, were added to the Ethospace line in 1988 as the system continued its evolution. These varied height cabinets can be freestanding or attached as support for partial-height walls. Storage components are available in solid color or recut veneer fronts, whereas overhead cabinet doors also have fabric/vinyl options. Work surfaces are offered in a selection of laminates and recut veneers.

Ethospace offices can be personalized from a selection of organizing tools including trays and shelves, as well as tackboards, mobile filing, and personal lights. The versatility of the system can also be applied to retail applications in store fixtures and display units.

Ethospace *managerial office interior with fabric-covered overhead storage and rich wood veneers.*

Ethospace support cabinets.

Burdick Group™

When Herman Miller introduced the Burdick Group in 1980, Bruce Burdick's freestanding desk system was hailed as "the ultimate desk." As an alternative to the traditional desk, Burdick designed a "workbench" on which the contemporary executive could arrange a unique assemblage of "work tools" to accommodate the high-tech office. The system is based on a series of components consisting of polished aluminum beams and cantilevered surfaces in a variety of shapes and sizes, which can be arranged for paper-intensive, computer-related, and conferencing activities. The components, including work surfaces, paper handling and storage elements, and electronic equipment supports, are located along a structural beam that can be configured to meet the precise requirements and changing work patterns of executives and professionals. The beam can be arranged in I-, T,- L-, or U- shaped configurations and is the heart of the wire management system. The black umber components are complemented by a selection of work surfaces available in glass, marble, laminate or wood. Although primarily intended for the workplace, the system can function elegantly in such diverse situations as corporate conference areas, executive or home dining rooms, and the home office.

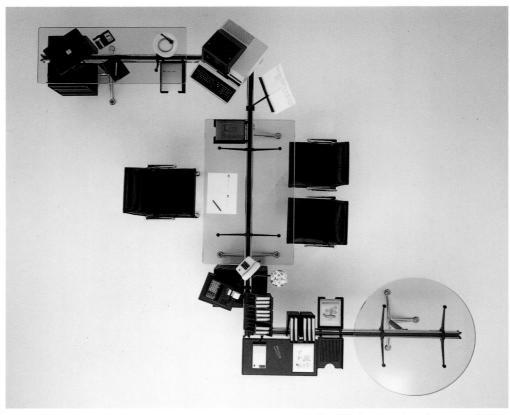

Burdick Group work surfaces are available in glass, marble, laminate or wood.

Burdick Group's freestanding desk system features cantilevered surfaces arranged on structural aluminum beams.

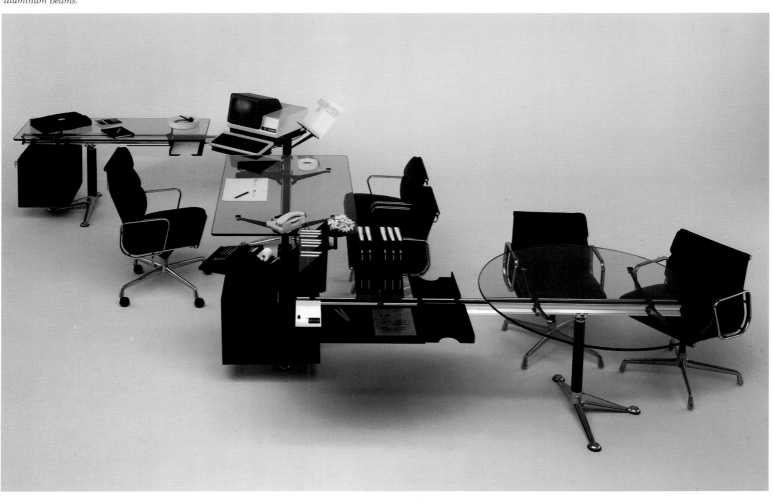

Newhouse Group® Furniture

The Newhouse Group of freestanding furniture, first introduced in 1987, serves both private and open offices with desks and components that stand alone or link to form workstations that continue the flow of work surface space. Links can join table desks and VDT tables or machine returns at 90, 120, or 135 degrees so that work surfaces can be of equal or unequal height and depth. Individual elements of the group were designed by Tom Newhouse for integration with existing Herman Miller systems, including Action Office, and Ethospace.

Newhouse Group components adapt to fit individual work styles and needs: the flying tool fence functions as both storage and a demarcation line between workstations; the bow-front cabinet can be fitted with file frames, coat bars and shelving; and the side car, with wheels attached for easy movement, can be used as a personal storage unit. Ease of configuration, efficient wire management, and a wide range of storage options contribute to its versatility.

The Newhouse Group is available in laminate finishes as well as veneers. The metal portions are color coordinated with the laminates and wood.

Newhouse Group office with computer cables managed through a trough in the modesty panels.

Newhouse Group in laminate with flying tool fences.

Relay® Furniture

Relay is a group of freestanding furniture that incorporates the emerging changes of the workplace into its game plan. Introduced by Herman Miller in 1990, Relay furniture was designed by Geoff Hollington to add adaptability and flexibility to the workplace environment. The collection consists of desks, tables, credenzas, interchangeable bookcases and shelves, with folding screens and bollards that can be used to define "territory" within the "boundaries" of the building architecture or an existing office landscape system. The system has homey design details such as spice drawers for small supplies, and teardrop-shaped tables for informal meetings.

Relay components stand alone, dock together and interface with other systems such as Newhouse Group and Ethospace Interiors. Its elements are adjustable to individual or group needs, and cable management is uncomplicated. Slides, glides, and casters enable easy rearrangement of the

pieces to create new meeting areas and spatial divisions. Visual and tactile interest is added by the combination of laminates, textured metals, and woods. Since it is designed and finished to be seen from every angle, Relay is equally versatile in private and open offices.

Development of Relay continued in 1991 with technology-supporting products bringing more options for energy distribution, computer integration and storage to the system. Included in those products are a powered end table, a cable pouch, and an adjustable high-performance desk/VDT table.

Relay table desk with adjustable surface and mobile puppy storage unit.

Relay height-adjustable desk and docking tear-drop table.

Relay freestanding furniture combined with high-energy capable Action Office Series 3 panels.

PANEL CONCEPTS

*Panel Concepts Inc. is headquartered in Santa
Ana, California, and is a wholly owned sub-
sidiary of Standard Pacific Corp. of Irvine,
California, a publicly traded company on the New
York Stock Exchange.*

Panel Concepts Furniture Systems

System Two.0, introduced in 1976, is a basic
metal system with a 2-inch wide panel, freestanding components, and laminate work surfaces. It is
available with or without electrical capabilities, or
electrical-ready for future power installation. System Two.0 cluster units can be arranged in groups
of two to six workstations. The unit's power is distributed from the central core to work surface
level or supplied directly from the base.

System Two.0's Shapes program consists of five
basic geometric work surfaces to create a variety
of configurations. Surface options are wood veneers and laminates.

The cost-effective System One.5 (1978) is a bare
bones metal panel system with 1½-inch thick
panels, panel-mounted storage and work surfaces, and no electrical capability.

Introduced in 1988, System Three.0 is a wood
system with 3-inch wide electrically-powered
panels in four profile options. Wood veneer components can be freestanding or panel-mounted.
For middle-to-upper management applications
there is a hybrid option of wood panels and metal
components with laminate work surfaces.

The Panel Concepts systems offer a range of
standard panel heights and widths as well as special curved and door panel styles. Panel surface
options include wood veneer, acoustical fabric,
and full or partially glazed. Storage options include full-size closets and pedestals, panel-
mounted overhead cabinets, shelves, trays and
drawer organizers.

System Two.0 managerial office.

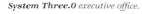

System Three.0 executive office.

System Two.0's Shapes program.

STEELCASE

The world's largest manufacturer of office furniture and furniture systems, Steelcase is a privately held, multinational company based in Grand Rapids, Michigan. Steelcase Strafor S.A. is headquartered in Strasbourg, Cedex, France, and Steelcase Japan Limited is in Tokyo, Japan.

Avenir™

Originally introduced in 1971 as Movable Walls, the system has undergone refinements and enhancements over the ensuing decades to reflect changes in the workplace. In 1990 the image and performance standards were so dramatically updated that Steelcase gave it a new name—Avenir™. This "foundation system" is built upon rational concepts: simplicity, flexibility, and accessibility. Avenir is a panel-based system, with compatible filing and storage components, and freestanding furniture elements available in a variety of materials and colors. Panel options include a selection of heights, surfaces, and acoustical properties. These elements can be integrated with freestanding desks, tables, credenzas, and cabinets to construct workstations and private offices. Avenir is made up of metal storage components available in 11 Steelcase colors with work surfaces in laminates and wood veneers. It is a moderately priced system that costs less than Steelcase's Series 9000.

Avenir workstations separated by panels to create privacy in an open plan office. Box drawers, lateral files, and open shelves foster maximum utilization of available space.

Avenir height-adjustable keyboard surface on panel-mounted work surface.

Series 9000®

The Series 9000 system is Steelcase's workhorse for the workplace. Since its introduction in 1973, it has undergone refinement, updating, and adaptation in response to changes in the office environment. These enhancements are designed to avoid obsolescence by integrating consistently with existing installations.

Rather than panel dependence, Series 9000 offers a modular approach that is stable in performance and flexible in design options. The system's characteristic "unit assembly" is the key to flexibility of reconfiguration since its freestanding furniture units can be moved independently of their panel enclosures. The same components can be used to create three types of office spaces: panel-supported, freestanding, or a combination of both. Working with such a design concept, a cantilevered work surface can become a freestanding unit and vice versa, or a panel-supported binder bin can be used with a freestanding desk. Whatever the choice, all the system's elements can be used to reflect corporate hierarchical levels through the selection of wood or laminate, fabric or paint finishes, in private or open office configurations.

Panels, nevertheless, play a significant role in the system's versatility and are available in both conventional and enhanced versions with the choice of tackable acoustical, transparent, and curved surfaces that are compatible electrically and mechanically. Visual interest can be added to the rectilinear landscape grid by using curved panels to create S-wall runs within conventional configurations. Enhanced panels consist of new steel frames with built-in base and top cavity, and replaceable surfaces on both sides. The enhanced panel surfaces include wood veneer, tackable acoustical, high-performance acoustical, or the three-piece TRI panel—tackable acoustical (T), receptacle access (R), internal storage (I).

The addition of Series 9000 accent panels to the product line in 1989 increases its long-term value by providing the ability to refurbish individual pieces of the office environment inexpensively without disrupting people or technology. The dimensional accent panels simply attach to Series 9000 conventional panels to add visual interest. They are sized to span either one or two conventional panels and are available in an enhanced selection of surface materials.

Although Series 9000 is essentially a metal system with work surfaces in laminate and veneer, its range reaches the executive level with the Valencia Wood Collection, a complete range of component and freestanding furniture in fine wood veneers.

Series 9000 professional-technical cluster.

Series 9000 height-adjustable single corner work surface.

Context®

Context is a freestanding office furniture system that can be built into a variety of work settings including open plan, private office, operation intensive or interactive team-based environments. Introduced in 1989, it is an innovative system designed within the "context" of the changing workplace. Its core units, the building blocks of the system, are curvilinear work surfaces to which privacy screens, utility elements, storage units, and accessories can be attached in multiple-choice configurations to support a balance between privacy and interaction.

Corner core units provide a refuge for individual activity, while other core units extend surfaces for tasks, conferences, team activities, and equipment support. Architecturally proportioned boundary walls and buttresses are used to create private areas in an open environment, and to define "macro" spaces for team identification and shared conferencing. Storage units including pedestals, dayfilers, lateral files, vertical cabinets and towers are all freestanding so they can be moved from place to place with ease. Overhead cabinets and privacy screens are column-mounted and can be added to any core unit.

Technology is integrated with independent utility elements that enable the placement of computers and peripherals anywhere on the units. Wire management is an integral part of the system, and change is simplified by the availability of power and data/telecommunications outlets at the base, as well as directly under and above the work surface.

The Context surface materials program was developed concurrently with the structural elements. Materials include laminate, and Silque®; a patented, non-glare work surface coating with a smooth, silky touch. Both work surface options are available in several colors. Component surfaces and accessories come in a variety of metals, coatings, and Mono-Tex paints (in 20 colors). There are also three composite veneers—cherry, rosewood, and birds-eye—in a selection of tones and colors. The independent boundary walls and removable privacy screens can be specified in several fabric lines or custom selected to create an exclusive look.

Context reception station.

Context enterprise table provides room to hold frequent meetings without disturbing work in progress on other surfaces.

Disney installation photos by Marius Rooks
Disney Direct Marketing Services, Inc.
The Walt Disney Company Designed by
Engel Picasso Associates, Chatham, New Jersey

Context spanner table with corner core unit and overhead storage cabinets.

Context undulating work surfaces accommodate right- or left-handed workers so they can shift their equipment accordingly.

Context *interactive islands for groups or teams are created with spanner tables attached to corner core units divided by core-mounted screens.*

Context *freestanding system divides space by core units, storage components and core-mounted screens.*

Ellipse

Ellipse is a contemporary desk system, created by Hans Werner, director of Stuttgart's Delta Design Group. It was first introduced in Europe by Steelcase Strafor and two years later, in 1990, by Steelcase, Inc. in the United States. The system offers a fine blend of high-aesthetics and high-tech. It is planned for design flexibility and can be configured for private offices, open spaces, team areas, receptionist stations, and specialized areas for technicians.

The foundation of Ellipse is the desk which accommodates its users with an ergonomically designed, sloped edge. Curved junction tops of 90 and 60 degrees provide for continuous, spacious work surfaces. Small round tables, strategically placed, help create informal discussion areas, while long rectangular conference tables are available for larger meetings. Low, tackable

screens give a modicum of privacy, whereas screens with shelf tops allow for over-the-counter transactions. Rails designed to hold the myriad desk accessories neatly organize the work surfaces. The system is accompanied by pedestals which come in freestanding, mobile and desk-mounted styles, as well as an assortment of high and low storage cabinets.

Vertical wire and cable management is incorporated into the legs; a horizontal power beam routes cabling through the workstations and is accessible from the user side of the work surface. Ellipse is a metal desking system available in 8 standard paint finishes including white, black, and neutral grays and beiges. There is a selection of 8 accent colors for the drawer hardware and leg trim. Work surfaces are offered in 7 laminates and 5 wood veneers.

Ellipse configuration featuring work surfaces created with junction tops, mobile pedestals, vertical storage cabinets and freestanding work tables.

Ellipse *multi-surface workstations, round confer-*
ence tables and vertical storage cabinets.

Ellipse *desk-mounted pedestal, storage cabinets*
and lateral files connected by a junction top.

TEKNION

Teknion Furniture Systems is a privately held company headquartered in Downsview, Ontario, Canada. Its United States operation, Teknion, Inc., is headquartered in Marlton, New Jersey. Teknion is a part of the Global Group of Companies, a loosely linked network of 18 corporations with interlocking financial interests, serving many different sectors of the office furniture field. Teknion International is based in Haifa Bay, Israel.

Teknion Office System

Stacking panels are the foundation of the Teknion Office System, designed by Ford and Earl in 1983. The steel-framed panel modules permit specifiers to create workstations of variable heights based upon the need for privacy or openness. Ceiling-high capability makes it possible to create enclosed, as well as open, office areas. The menu of interchangeable panels includes: standard panels in acoustic and non-acoustic versions, both straight and radiused; power panels for significant power management; plus a group of special panels to perform specialized functions. Panel inserts are available in wood veneers, glazed, and fabric finishes.

The system's signature horizontal band of hinged access doors on both sides of the panel put the power at work surface height and at arm's reach. The system has an advanced raceway system that can handle, distribute, and access high voltage power and communications cables, as well as fiber optics. Fiber optics and the peripheral equipment that goes with it, can be housed within the protection of the panel, out of harm's way. The snap-off panel covers provide ready access to data and communication cabling within the panel cavity.

Teknion executive office with fabric-finished panels and overhead storage.

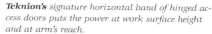

Teknion's signature horizontal band of hinged access doors puts the power at work surface height and at arm's reach.

The off-module component attachment increases the ability to tailor workspaces to meet specific needs so the component doesn't have to adhere to the panel module. This ability to position hanging components from horizontal rails makes it possible to use varied planning grids on opposite sides of a panel, and to use existing components when workstations are reconfigured. Work surface configurations include: standard, curvilinear, and piano-, bullet- and P-shaped tops in laminate and wood. Work surfaces are available in three versions: panel-supported, semi-suspended and freestanding. Specialized work surfaces include: five-sided corner, rectangular EDP, and radiused corner for use with radiused panels; counter tops mounted on acoustical panels for reception and secretarial areas; and adjustable keyboard surfaces.

Storage components consist of steel, wood, or self-skinning urethane-fronted pedestals, and steel, wood or fabric-covered open and closed hanging overheads. Pedestals are available as freestanding furniture or as work surface suspended. The Provider, a multi-purpose steel cabinet with recess doors, is suitable for storage, wardrobe and electronic computer equipment. It is available in three heights with steel, wood or fabric doors.

Two lines of freestanding furniture—Freestanding Laminate Furniture (1988) and Libretto (1989)—and a Steel Storage line, purchased from Croydon Office Furniture in 1990, are all aesthetically compatible with the Teknion Office System.

Libretto, in wood veneer, includes work surfaces, credenzas, and a variety of storage, such as pedestals and cabinets. Work surfaces are available in various configurations such as bullet- and P-shaped tops.

Teknion semi-suspended unit with curvilinear, piano- and bullet-shaped work surfaces and intermediate shelf.

Teknion workstations with varied panel heights.

Teknion's work organizer element replaces a regular acoustic panel and holds a paper management accessory system.

TRENDWAY

Trendway is a privately held company, headquartered in Holland, Michigan.

Choices™

Introduced in 1991, Choices builds on the proven panel system, SMS. It is a single system with a contemporary look and greater adaptability in rectilinear, curved or cluster configurations. To create open and private offices, Choices can be easily integrated with TrendWall's floor-to-ceiling partitions to create interactive or private office areas. Components include work surfaces, overhead storage units, shelves, suspended and free-standing pedestals, lateral file units, tables, and freestanding desks. The system also offers wood styling with wood trim panels (top and end caps) and work surfaces in three wood veneers: mahogany, cherry and oak.

The Choices panel has been re-engineered to incorporate a rolled-formed steel frame, and to offer increased acoustical abilities. Its PowerPac™ 8-wire electrical system, in the base-mounted cableway, offers increased power capabilities to the standard electrical system.

Panels are available in a selection of heights with optional pass-throughs, curved and glazed panels, and doors. Choices is essentially as cost-effective as Trendway's Space Management System. The company prides itself on its Trendway Xpress three-day shipping program.

Choices *semi-private workstation setting with conferencing capabilities.*

Choices *curvilinear work surfaces promote active sharing.*

UNIFOR, Inc.

UNIFOR is the contract division of the Molteni Group, a major European furniture company. UNIFOR, Inc. is headquartered in Long Island City, New York, and is the American arm of the privately held company based in Turate (Como), Italy.

Misura ST

Designed by Luca Meda and introduced in 1986, Misura ST is a line of freestanding workstations with work surfaces that can be height adjusted with a hand-crank mechanism to accommodate electronic equipment, or accessorized with computer and printer support units. To insure privacy, the workstations can be divided with suspended upholstery or aluminum screens at various heights. The screens are designed to accommodate paper management accessories. The I Satelliti, computer support units, in integral melamine provide additional work space for group tasks as well as additional work surfaces. Tops are available in lengths of 29½ to 108½ inches in gray plastic laminate or oak veneers, at two standard depths of 29½ and 23⅝ inches. Storage pedestals are painted and edge-banded particle board. For an open plan solution, the freestanding workstations can be specified with Pannelli PL panels for full enclosure or with a central spine to accommodate overhead storage and shelves.

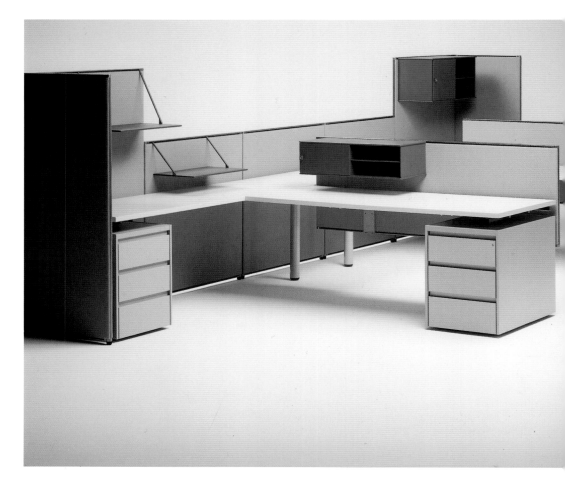

Misura ST structural legs in stamped and extruded aluminum complete with wire management and height adjustment; suspended screens upholstered in fabric and complete with aluminum profiles to accommodate hanging storage.

66

Misura ST casegoods in painted and edge-banded high density particle board.

Misura ST workstations with a series of modular panels that can be used alone or coordinated with suspended panels, available in upholstered or glazed versions.

Misura ST and *Mood* are both compatible with Unifor's freestanding storage system.

Mood

Although each piece has its own character and can stand on its own, the shared details and definite dimensional affinity of the desks, tables, cabinets, and accessories that comprise the Mood system make it a family of furniture, rather than a rigid system. Designed in 1987 by Fernando Urquijo and Giorgio Macola for an American corporate headquarters in Europe, the system's quality of design detail and the sensitive choice of materials are in the tradition of fine furniture. The warm and luxurious light wood veneer work surfaces are an elegant contrast with Mood's sand-blasted bases and polished gunmetal columns. The ergonomic shape of the desk edge slopes to conform to its user's arms. Suspended or freestanding panels are aluminum with horizontal profiles to support storage elements. The system has external wire management capabilities. The Mood line is suited for use in private offices or in open-plan areas where it can be supplemented by: suspended screens, Pannelli PL, and Progetto 25.

Mood work surfaces supported by a combination of support and storage elements with bridge return and suspended aluminum panel.

Mood semi-circular table desk supplemented with freestanding storage.

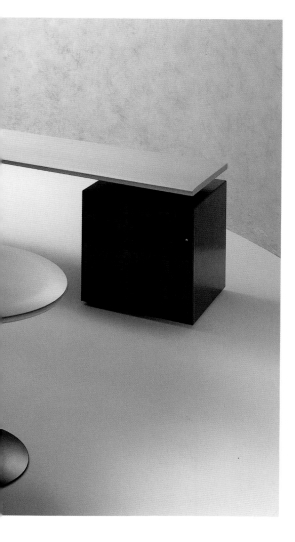

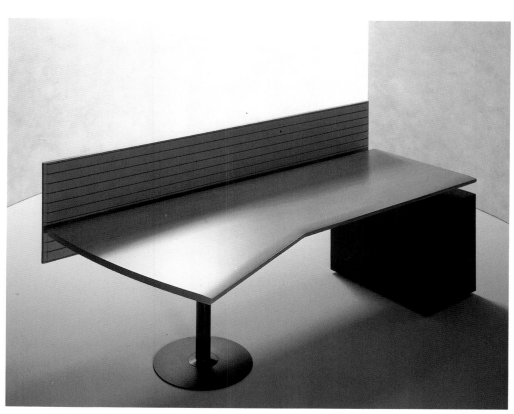

Mood butterfly-shaped conferencing work surface supports suspended aluminum screen with profiles to accommodate storage and accessory options.

Mood table desks in a range of shapes, sizes and finishes with freestanding executive credenza.

Pannelli PL

Pannelli PL panels, designed by Luca Meda in 1989, are well suited to dividing space in an open plan situation. The modular panels surround the Misura and Mood freestanding furniture rather than support it. Panel depth is only 1½ inches, so creepage is kept to a minimum. The panels are available upholstered in various textiles, as glazed panels with three standard glass tints, or as combination upholstered/glazed panels. They are universal for ease of installation and reconfiguration. Hinged joints between panels rotate 180 degrees at 15-degree intervals. Enclosed overhead storage, shelves with or without task lighting, and other accessories such as rotating computer supports are easily mounted and demounted. Since the panels are independent from the furniture, storage and accessory placement is not limited by panel module. The panels can be used for full enclosure, or as a central spine with workstations divided by aluminum or upholstered suspended screens.

Pannelli PL panels are ideal for achieving a freer open plan to accommodate group interactive tasks, while maintaining a private environment for individual work needs. They are available in four heights (42¹¹⁄₃₂ to 70⅞ inches) and in six widths (23⅝ to 47¼ inches). The panel frames are extruded aluminum with an internal structure of perforated steel and sound-absorbing material. Vertical communication channels are designed so wires can exit from the channel at varied heights to feed and connect the hardware above and below the desktop. Three types of channels allow the horizontal distribution and management of wires.

Pannelli PL hinged joints between panels rotate at 180 degree intervals.

Pannelli PL external profiles of extruded aluminum accommodate hanging storage and connection of panels at various heights.

Progetto 25

Progetto 25 is a technology wall, designed by Luca Meda in 1990, that carries the communication and electrical requirements for Misura ST and Mood. It is a major "almost" architectural wall in terms of function and scale which acts as a transitional element between the building and the furniture. For appropriate flexibility, the wall and furniture can function independently of each other. The wall is 5 inches deep, and wall height is modular in 9⅞-inch modules, with a minimum height of 40½ inches and a maximum of 118⅛ inches. An area above the work surface is dedicated to wire management, or the wall can be hard-wired. The profiles between the horizontal facades are designed to receive other elements such as panels, smaller scale walls, hanging shelves, overhead storage, accessories, etc. Since the Progetto wall can take such assorted finishes as plaster, paint, upholstery fabric, or vinyl, surface variations can help to define diverse areas. Material finishes can be varied on either facade of the wall, to help define collective zones from individual work areas, corridors from an open plan, and private rooms from service areas. Each part takes its logic from the elements of architecture.

Progetto 25 wall characterized by a horizontal profile adapted for continuous connection of suspended accessories and panels.

Progetto 25 technologically intelligent wall functions as a transition between the architecture and the furniture.

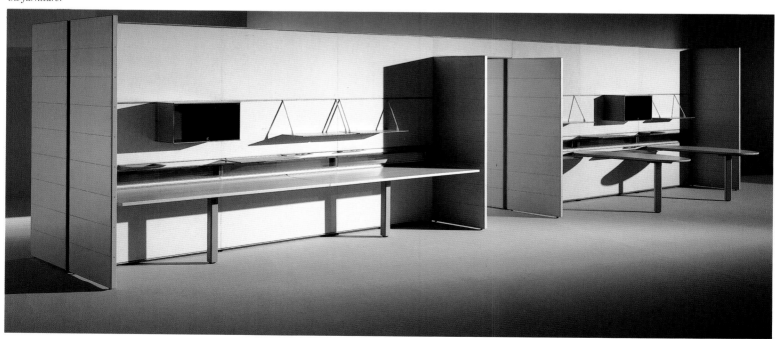

VOKO U.S., INC.

VOKO U.S., Inc. is located in Pittsburgh, Pennsylvania. VOKO Franz Vogt & Co., KG in Giessen, Germany, is the parent company and the largest producer of office furniture in Germany.

Univers V-10

Introduced in the fall of 1988, Univers V-10 is a freestanding beam-based modular office system. The "core" of the system is an extruded aluminum beam which acts as the support and slideway for all its components. It can be specified in custom lengths to best fit any specified application. The beam, rectangular in cross section, enables system components to be bolted to any of its four sides: leg columns, in four styles with various bases, attach to the beam's bottom edge; a variety of work surfaces supported by cantilevered brackets attach to its top edge; and optional cable management modules attach to its back edge. The system offers height-adjustable work surfaces: an automatic-assisted surface that travels up to 44 inches high, and a manual hand-crank surface with a 6-inch range of 26 to 32 inches. Like most systems, Univers is designed to manage the power and cabling requirements of the modern electronic office. Vertical and horizontal cable ducts and optional triplex outlets bring power to the worktop and eliminate cable clutter. The system integrates with modular freestanding VOKO storage components which include pedestals, cabinets, lateral files, and credenzas available in steel, laminate and wood veneer. It is the vast range of freestanding storage options, special height-adjustable modules, and the inherent simplicity of the beam that enables Univers V-10 to change and grow as businesses evolve. To add a "vertical" dimension to workstation design, freestanding Univers V-10 workmodule configurations can be combined with panels from the VOKO RMT system.

Univers V-10's beam and leg elements are aluminum, heavy gauge steel and brass, and are available in a wide palette of standard paint colors. Work surface options include laminate, veneer, glass or natural stone.

Univers V-10 *data workstation corner unit with panel system.*

Univers V-10 *cantilevered bracket attaches to the beam.*

Univers V-10 *configuration with glass and height-variable worktops.*

CHAPTER TWO

OFFICE SEATING SYSTEMS

Executive, Managerial/Professional, Task, General Office

There are eight essential features to consider when selecting office seating: durability, cost, comfort, space savings, safety, availability and ergonomics. Of these characteristics, ergonomics presents the specifier with the most latitude and, in some instances, the greatest perplexity.

Industry research has shown the significantly positive impact of ergonomics on productivity, efficiency, and health factors in the workplace. When long-term seating is an issue, the right chair can lead to a reduction in time lost due to worker injuries and the costs associated with medical expenses and worker compensation claims. The effect on seating specification is both to complicate and simplify the selection process: the variety of types and models is enormous, yet industry standards and state legislation result in categories and guidelines that leave design professionals and facility managers small margins of error.

Ergonomic seating is designed to give optimal support with minimum stress on the spine while reducing fatigue of the back, shoulder, thigh, leg, and arm muscles. Essentially there are two types of ergonomic chairs: active and passive. Active ergonomic chairs feature manual controls that the sitter can adjust to a preferred comfort level and then lock into place. The user must activate the controls which include seat, back and sometimes arm height adjustments. Chairs also provide backrest tension control with some type of back stop that the user can set at a desired angle. Passive ergonomic chairs have seat and backrest angles that are linked to move in sync with the user's body movements in a constantly changing interactive relationship between the user and the chair. Passive chairs also offer seat height adjustment and backrest tension control, usually with some sort of back lock.

Chairs generally come in unified collections with specific classifications that often describe the user's position and function within the corporation. However, as the of-

fice and technology change, so do workers' needs. As a result, basic office chair classifications are starting to be drawn more along task rather than position lines. Although there are four basic ergonomic chair categories reflecting corporate standing and task levels, there is an increased acceptance of crossover applications.

Executive chairs have high backs and are more impressive than seating for the rest of the office. Visual appeal, size, status and comfort are important considerations. CEO or top level executives are often in a leaning-back-in-the-chair consulting mode and may be moderate keyboard users. Executive chairs account for the smallest portion of the seating market.

Managerial/professional or high-performance office chairs usually have mid- to high-backs and are for upper managers who perform multi-tasks such as meeting, phone, and computer work. Professionals, such as writers and draftsman, who are task-inten-

sive and not especially multi-functional, should select a chair that is more related to work applications.

Task or operator chairs usually have low backs, but there is a tendency in the industry to add higher ones to increase back support for people who work at computers regularly. Dedicated-task workers, such as telephone operators and telemarketers, perform repetitive tasks and therefore require more stability. Adjustability is important to these workers because they need to change positions periodically to stay healthy. To reduce fatigue they require comfortable chairs that offer seat and back height adjustments, as well as height-adjustable arms. Task chairs for VDT users should meet ANSI/HFS 100-1988 standards for seating. One of the most critical ANSI/HFS standards is seat height adjustability which requires a movement range of 4½ inches, from 16 to 20½ inches.

General Office or basic performance chairs have medium or high backs and are for people who don't sit for extended periods of

time, but are often in and out of their chairs. Basic ergonomic support is sufficient for people who, when seated, perform multi-tasks moving from telephone to paperwork to computer keyboard throughout the work day.

The American National Standards Institute (ANSI), headquartered in New York City, first published guidelines for office furniture suited to video display terminal (VDT) use in 1988. These guidelines, researched and published by The Human Factors Society, Inc., set standards for a worker's physical placement and interaction with computer equipment. The ANSI guidelines address adjustability as it relates to field of vision, seating posture, work surface, monitor/VDT height and keyboard positioning. Currently there is legislation, based mainly on the ANSI standards, that addresses these adjustability issues. In various locales legislation has already been passed or is still being formulated. The fact is that these guidelines may provide the keys to creating a happier, healthier workplace.

Important features to look for when specifying chairs:

- Mechanical or pneumatic-lift controls to provide precise seat height adjustment

- Adjustable-height backrest or a well-contoured backrest with lumbar support

- Adjustable tilt tension control

- Locking posture control of backrest angles as a comfort option

- Limited front seat rise that permits the occupant to recline yet allows feet to stay flat on the floor with knees bent at a 90-degree angle so thigh circulation isn't constricted and the viewing angle remains level

- Height-adjustable arms as a comfort factor depending on user's size

- Molded foam seat

- All chairs should swivel—if the chair twists your back doesn't have to twist

- A sturdy five-point base prevents easy tip-over

- Chairs should meet general ANSI-BIFMA standards for reliability and safety, and ANSI/HFS 100-1988 standards for VDT users

Other considerations when selecting an office chair:

- Special fire code seating to meet fire code standards such as fire-retardant versions that pass the Boston Fire Code, California Code 133, and New York Port Authority requirement. Chairs must be manufactured with special cushions and upholstered in approved fabrics to meet specific flammability and/or contamination factors—especially useful for densely populated office buildings, public areas, and healthcare facilities.

- Anti-microbial vinyls and fabrics, treated to cut down on the transfer of germs, can be especially important for multi-shift operators. Special formulations are built into material to make it resistant to attack by microbes. Health care institutions especially prefer these germ-resistant materials.

- Green factors are being incorporated into chairs by several manufacturers to make them friendly to the environment. Environmentally safe seating is produced with non-contaminating or recyclable materials to help reduce the pollution of our earth.

Office chairs come in a wide selection of fabrics and leathers, but in many cases there is no limit to what can be specified by the customer. In the industry this is referred to as COM (customer's own material) or COL (customer's own leather).

Here are the best chairs designed to satisfy the most discriminating sitters whatever their body type, job or title. They either meet, or if necessary can be modified to meet, the ANSI HFS/100-1988 ergonomic standards for seating. Make sure to get the manufacturer to verify compliance.

Persona & Persona Plus

DESIGNER   Mario Bellini/Dieter Thiel

MANUFACTURER   Vitra Seating Inc.
Allentown, Pennsylvania

MATERIALS   Both models come mono-colored, or with contrasting color gussets that cover the lateral supports where the chair flexes. Variety of fabrics and leathers available. The Persona Plus chairs have thicker upholstery, deeper seats and higher backs. Bases: charcoal-colored polypropylene with optional leg-end covers available in charcoal aluminum, or polished chrome. COM/COL.

The Persona task chair is suited to heavy computer work. The Persona Plus is a managerial/professional chair that can also function in the conference room. In both models, the gussets mark the pivot point for all body movements. The chair hugs its sitter around the lower back where it's most needed. Both chairs are self-adjusting, on constant free float—how much weight is on the seat determines how much tension or flex there is on the backrest. An adjustment knob under the seat tightens or loosens back tension. A pneumatic gas cylinder regulates height adjustment and provides a smooth ride up and down. Arms are removable in the field. Chair cushions come off as one piece and are field replaceable.

AC 1 & AC 2

DESIGNER Antonio Citterio

MANUFACTURER Vitra Seating Inc.
Allentown, Pennsylvania

MATERIALS Available in selected Vitra
fabrics and leathers. AC 2 offers optional
Girard black-and-white checked fabric.
Approved COM/COL.

The AC 1 is for task to upper management,
and the AC 2 is for upper management. The
AC 1 chair has an 18-inch-wide task seat.
The chair is notable for the interesting tension between its seat and back. The shape
of the backrest and its support point have
been designed so that the lower lumbar region is always correctly supported. The
seat conforms to the sitter's body. AC 2 has
broad surfaces yet a slim appearance.

Imago

DESIGNER   Mario Bellini/Dieter Thiel

MANUFACTURER   Vitra Seating Inc.
Allentown, Pennsylvania

MATERIALS   Available in a full range of
Vitra fabrics or leathers. COM/COL

An upper management/executive armchair,
Imago is available in standard or medium
height, high-back with adjustable headrest, and conference/visitor sled-base
armchair in standard or medium-height
back. Imago has a wider seat and back
than Figura, with thicker foam cushioning
and fully upholstered leather arms. Swivel
chairs have a synchronized seat mechanism that maintains the ideal angle
between seat and back. All chairs have upholstered foam and fiberfill lumbar belt,
with charcoal or chrome buckle to match
the base. Pneumatic height adjustment
and a variable stop/go control allows back
to be locked at desired angle.

Figura

DESIGNER Mario Bellini/Dieter Thiel

MANUFACTURER Vitra Seating Inc.
Allentown, Pennsylvania

MATERIALS Chair covers are changeable
to allow for dry cleaning, or change in
office color scheme. Non-removable
upholstery also available in the task/
managers seating. Available in 1, 2, or 3
different colors in a wide variety of Vitra
fabrics and leathers. High-back executive
chair available only in non-removable upholstery. COM/COL.

A task to middle management chair, Figura
is available in standard or high-back versions, as well as conference/visitor
cantilevered, or with a four-leg base. Its
synchronized seating mechanism, which
maintains the ideal angle between seat
and back, promotes active sitting. Pneumatic height adjustment and a variable
stop/go control allows back to be locked at
desired angle. Artistic use of colors and
materials gives it a congenial, less bureau-
cratic appearance.

Kita

DESIGNER Toshiyuki Kita

MANUFACTURER ICF
Orangeburg, New York

MATERIALS Shell: injection-molded, steel-reinforced polyurethane covered with molded foam can be upholstered to specification. COM/COL. Base: black rigid polyurethane-coated steel; executive models also available in black epoxied aluminum with polished aluminum or chrome top cap.

Ergodynamically designed, Kita's task and standard models are offered with an optional articulating back; the executive model is available only with a self-articulating back. The pneumatic height adjustment has a mechanism that allows the chair to tilt or be in a fixed position. There are two executive versions: the executive with or without the headrest, and the executive high-back. A sled-base armchair rounds out the line.

System 28

DESIGNER Simon Desanta

MANUFACTURER Comforto®, A Haworth Portfolio Company
Holland, Michigan

MATERIALS Standard bases come in 5 basic colors with polypropylene or optional chrome protective caps. Wide selection of textiles and leathers for this extensive family of fully-upholstered chairs. COM/COL. Wood trim option (arms and base) for upscale office needs.

System 28 is a complete line of functionally designed ergonomic seating including executive, management, operational, stacking, and pedestal or sled-base conference chairs. All of the chairs have fully-upholstered outer shells for design continuity from the executive suite to the training room. The outward curve of the lower back is designed for optimal back support. Standard features include pneumatic seat height adjustment, and a knee-tilt recline mechanism with locking posture control. To complement the System 28 line, Comforto also offers System 27, a task chair with a polypropylene shell and basic knee-tilt mechanism with lock, at a more economical price point.

System 18 Seating
Solutions

MANUFACTURER   Comforto®, A Haworth
Portfolio Company
Holland, Michigan

MATERIALS   Polypropylene or optional
fully-upholstered outer shell. Steel base
with polypropylene or optional chrome
scuff guards.Wide range of Haworth and
Comforto fabrics and leathers as well as
COM/COL.

This chair system was specifically designed
to meet the ANSI/HFS standards. System
18 runs the full gamut, from executive to
operational chair and stool. The task and
professional chair offer precise adjustment
of the lumbar back support to relieve muscle tension and strain on the spinal
column. The standard bio-synchronized
mechanism locks in 6 positions. Comforto
has mechanical or pneumatic seat height
adjustment and field retrofittable arms. Adjustable arms are optional.

Ergon 2®

DESIGNER   Bill Stumpf

MANUFACTURER   Herman Miller
Zeeland, Michigan

MATERIALS   Integral-color polypropylene
seat and back outer shells to match frame
finishes, or upholstered to match cushion.
Bases and armrests are die-cast aluminum.
Upholstery in a wide range of fabrics, vinyl,
and leather. COM/COL.

Ergon 2 is the updated version of the
Ergon chair (the first chair in the United
States to be designed based on ergonomics), designed by Bill Stumpf in 1976.
Adjustments for seat height, back height,
tilt tension, and arm height tailor the Ergon
2 chair to the person who uses it—in scale
and in function. A knob adjusts the task
chair's back by controlling its angle, and by
moving it to change the depth of the seat-
pan. The forward angle of the seat-pan
can be adjusted 5 degrees, and a synchronized, knee-tilt mechanism includes an
adjustable tilt lock. Seat and back edges
are comfortably rounded whether they are
on task, executive or management chairs,
or stools. Independent height-adjustable
arms are available and can be retrofitted
to upgrade existing models. An optional
foot pillow of high density, urethane foam,
ranges from 1½ inches at the front to 5¼
inches at the back edge.

Equa®

DESIGNER   Bill Stumpf and Don Chadwick

MANUFACTURER   Herman Miller
Zeeland, Michigan

MATERIALS   One-piece, flexible, injection-molded, glass-reinforced thermoplastic polyester (Rynite) shell in a range of colors. Bases and armrests are die-cast aluminum. Upholstery in a wide range of fabric, vinyl, and leather. COM/COL.

The H-shaped cutout between the seat and back permits all parts of Equa to flex independently of each other, and allows air to circulate and cool the body. Ergonomic responsiveness is built into this basic office chair. On most models, all the user needs to adjust is the height and tilt tension. Soft and curved edges add comfort, while the front sloped seat helps circulation to the legs and feet. A dwell mechanism keeps the user upright until weight is shifted back. The tilt pivot is located behind the knees instead of above the center column, so when leaning back the sitter's feet stay on the floor. The line includes: low- and high-back work chairs, with or without arms, in five-star, sled base and rocker options; plus operational stools, with optional tilt pivot control and adjustable-height foot rings, so the user can sit at a stand-up work surface. Equa is lightweight and mobile with arms comfortably wide and sloped in front making it easier to get closer to work surfaces. Field replaceable cushions are available on split pad models. Independent height-adjustable arms are an option and can be retrofitted to upgrade existing models.

Wilkhahn FS+ Series

DESIGNER Klaus Franck and
Werner Sauer

MANUFACTURER Vecta, member Steelcase
Design Partnership
Grand Prairie, Texas

MATERIALS Swivel 5-prong base of one-piece die-cast aluminum. Sled base tubular frame of 14-gauge steel, 1 inch in diameter. Bases available in polished aluminum, mirrored chrome, hammered pewter, fused-bronze or thermoset finish. Seats upholstered over steel frame. Molded polyurethane foam inner structure is embedded with elastic webbing for comfort. Two upholstery options: smooth or horizontal ribbing at the lower center back or across the entire seat and back. Upholstery: Vecta fabrics, vinyl, leather and approved COM/COL.

This series of ergonomic chairs ranges from Grand Class executive through managerial to operational and sled-base guest chairs. Each has pneumatic height adjustment and automatic synchro-tilt for constant lumbar support. Tension control regulates ease of tilt movement. An optional locking tab mechanism fixes tilt chairs in position. A footstool is also available.

90

Cadet

DESIGNER   Gerd Lange

MANUFACTURER   Vecta, member Steelcase
Design Partnership
Grand Prairie, Texas

MATERIALS   Single section cushion of
multi-density contoured foam. Upholstery
cover clips to seat shell of polypropylene.
Base finish in black only. Arms: black polypropylene or leather. Upholstery: Vecta
fabrics, vinyl, leather and approved
COM/COL.

Cadet is a general office and conference
room chair with seat and backrest formed
from a flexible, single section shell. Mid-
and low-back models are available. It offers pneumatic height adjustment and a
tilt mechanism with an adjustable tension
control that regulates ease of tilt movement. A locking tab mechanism enables
the chair to be fixed in working position.
Sled base chairs have a low, flexible backrest with an oval-shaped tubular black
frame. A drafter's chair is available with
fixed mid-back, swivel and height adjustment. Cadet was initially introduced to
Europe by Steelcase/Strafor.

4 O'Clock

DESIGNER   Jeff Cronk

MANUFACTURER   Vecta, member Steelcase
Design Partnership
Grand Prairie, Texas

MATERIALS   Cast aluminum base in polished aluminum and standard Vecta thermoset colors. Upholstery includes leather,
enhanced by stitching detail and perforated
leather panel, and Vecta fabrics. Back panel
can be specified in different fabric.
COM/COL.

The 4 O'Clock chair provides an egalitarian
solution to seating an entire organization
with one visual statement and two ergonomic mechanisms, A.M. and P.M. Both
mechanisms comply with the ANSI/HFS
100-1988 standards. A.M., or Active Mechanism, for VDT operators, has a lever that
easily adjusts the independent seat/back
angle and locks it into the desired position.
P.M., or Passive Mechanism, for multi-task
workers, has a sophisticated tilting mechanism that offers a dynamic seat and back
motion. A knob under the seat allows the
user to adjust tilt tension, and a separate
front suspension mechanism offers zero
front rise. There are two sizes in each A.M.
and P.M. model. Both models have width-
and height-adjustable arms. Adjustable
back heights are optional. There is a
choice of mechanical or pneumatic height
adjustments. The 4 O'Clock chair is so
named because it is meant to feel as comfortable at 4 o'clock as it did at 9 o'clock.

Sensor®

DESIGNER Wolfgang Muller-Deisig

MANUFACTURER Steelcase
Grand Rapids, Michigan

MATERIALS Choice of light and dark colors for shells and bases. Available in a wide range of fabrics and leathers as well as COM/COL.

Sensor is a high performance general office chair for multi-task jobs such as meetings, phone, and computer work. The line extends to mid- and high-back desk chairs, high and low stools, guest and conference chairs, and sled-base side chairs. Since the chair senses body movement and moves with the body providing continuous self-adjustment, Sensor needs only two manual adjustments: seat height and backrest tension. The seat height adjusts from 16 to 21 inches, and the backrest tension control is available with a variable back stop option. Sculptured cushioning has contours that conform to the body and help to distribute weight properly. Three different arm styles are available: omega, T, and fully-enclosed. Three different chair sizes accommodate a range of body sizes as well as professional levels.

Criterion™

DESIGNER   Zooey Chu and Steelcase
Project Team
MANUFACTURER   Steelcase
Grand Rapids, Michigan
MATERIALS   The chair back and base cap
come in scuff-resistant engineering plastic
for maximum durability. Upholstery available in a wide range of fabrics and colors
including COM/COL.

Criterion chairs and stools are appropriate
for task-intensive jobs. Lots of adjustments
are available so chairs can be tailored to
people and their tasks. The flick of a switch
turns the operational model into a continuous tilt chair for multi-task work and just
as easily returns it to a stable support
chair for task-intensive use. There's also a
high-back version which offers upper back
support as well as a way to differentiate
status levels. Seat height adjustment
ranges from 15½ to 20½ inches with a
manual or optional pneumatic height control. The seat tilt range is from minus 5
to plus 8 degrees. Back tilt ranges from
minus 3 to plus 16 degrees and offers
locked-in back support. The critical trunk-
thigh angle is never less than 92 degrees.
Back height adjustment is 2 inches, and
width of arms can be adjusted by 2 inches.
Other arm adjustments are available: a
synchronized arm height adjustment with a
range of 2 inches, and an independent arm
height adjustment with a range of 4
inches.

94

Rally™

DESIGNER Bruce Smith

MANUFACTURER Steelcase
Grand Rapids, Michigan

MATERIALS Monochromatic finished
frame. A variety of fabrics and colors including COM/COL. Options include: sewn
leather upholstery, upholstered arm caps,
and chrome base caps.

Rally is a reasonably priced, basic performance, general office chair suitable for
people who don't have to sit all day. It is
not geared to high-performance, ergonomic
applications as are its Steelcase relatives,
Sensor and Criterion. Rally seating includes
high-back and mid-back desk chairs with or
without arms, and a sled-base, mid-back
side chair with arms. Its twisted ribbon-like
arms add an attractive dimension. Desk
chairs offer swivel tilt technology with no
front rise so the user can recline but still
keep two feet on the ground. Seat height
and tension adjustments can adapt to any
worker. Rally is cushion contoured and has
field replaceable arms and cushions.

Arena

DESIGNER   Sumner Adams and Kimball
design staff

MANUFACTURER   Kimball International
Jasper, Indiana

MATERIALS   Polypropylene shell and base.
Finish options: midnight black and taupe
gray. Upholstery options: Kimball fabric or
leather. Maharam textiles. COM/COL.

Arena is a complete line of chairs including
desk and side chairs with sinuous curved
arms. Other models are used as general
office seating for multi-task use. The optional SoftArc knee pivot control offers a
smooth ride for upright and reclining positions and eliminates pressure under legs
from the seat's front edge when the user is
in a reclining position. A dwell mechanism
in the pivot control supports the user in the
upright position yet provides full support,
to reduce tension, when reclining. Arena
has field-installable and replaceable arms.
The VDT task chair offers height-adjustable
T arms.

Consens Revival

DESIGNER   Fritz Makiol

MANUFACTURER   Girsberger Industries
Smithfield, North Carolina

MATERIALS   Aluminum base. Shell is
Luran S (BASF) a styrene-acrylonitrile
copolymer. Consens shell: sandy gray, dark
brown, and black. Consens Revival shell:
platinum gray, and black. Removable cushions may be upholstered in Girsberger
fabrics, or COM/COL.

Consens Revival is the updated 1989 version of the Consens chair, designed in
1972. Revival offers a more modern base
and sloping arms. Both collections consist
of swivel desk chairs in high- and low-back-
rest models with companion guest chairs.
Chairs are scaled to two different sizes—I
smaller secretarial/task, and II wider managerial—and offer two motion adjustment
choices: in the CI model the seat and
backrest are individually adjustable and
the backrest/lumbar support is height adjustable; in the CS model, the seat and
backrest synchronically follow the body's
movements. Both versions offer seat
height adjustment via the touch of a button. Adjustable-height arms are optional. A
drafting stool configuration is also
available.

Flexis ™

DESIGNER   Jonathan Ginat

MANUFACTURER   United Chair
Leeds, Alabama

MATERIALS   Five frame finishes: black,
charcoal, char-brown, medium gray, and
beige. Available fully upholstered, or with
plastic shell back. Upholstery available in
broad range of fabrics, colors, and leather.
COM/COL.

The Flexis line offers executive medium-
and high-back, operational, and sled-base
guest chairs, plus management and
operational stools. Dual pivot design incorporates a knee-tilt control and back
pivot, allowing the seat control and back
mechanisms to act simultaneously yet independently to provide a wide range of
movement (20 degrees of seat pivot, 17
degrees of back pivot). The knee-tilt control
mechanism adjusts to accommodate a
broad range of body sizes, from 95 to 250
pounds. Properly positioned lumbar support
eliminates the need for back height adjustment. Executive and operational models
feature standard pneumatic seat height
adjustment, or an optional spin-lift
mechanism.

BodyBilt™

MANUFACTURER   The Chair Works
College Station, Texas

MATERIALS   Steel frame. Contoured seats with multi-layered variable densities of foam. Upholstery options: wide range of fabrics and colors, Finesse (vinyl substitute), and leather. COM/COL.

BodyBilt is a task chair with nine standard adjustments. The pneumatic seat height offers a 5-inch range, and the front and rear seat tilt adjusts plus or minus 7.5 degrees and locks at any selected angle. The back height moves 2.5 inches on .5-inch increments to position lumbar support for the lower back; the back angle functions independently of the seat tilt, with a 30-degree adjustment. The lumbar area features standard lumbar roll cushioning, and an optional inflatable air lumbar pillow. Three-way adjustable arms offer: a 3-inch range of height adjustment, a 3-inch range of width adjustment, and a full 360-degree swivel. Arm adjustability is designed to accommodate many tasks, especially computer keyboarding, and relieves strain on the neck/shoulder area as well as helping maintain proper forearm support. For special applications, linear tracking arms will "retrofit" to the standard arm bracket, and can be attached on one or both arms. An optional back depth adjustment can offer up to a 2-inch longer seat depth for very tall users.

Bulldog™

DESIGNERS   Dale Fahnstrom & Michael McCoy

MANUFACTURER   The Knoll Group
New York, New York

MATERIALS   Select upholstery from over 75 standard Knoll Textile fabrics and a broad selection of Spinneybeck leathers. The spectrum of colors gives the specifier over 1,500 covering choices. COM/COL. Base, arm and back shell colors are integrally colored to hide wear and tear.

Bulldog offers one- or two-piece seat forms; eight models with or without arms; four adjustment control packages to equip any model. The Basic 1 and 2 control packages are for people who engage in varied activities; the Advanced control package, which offers a forward tilt and variable position tilt lock, is for dedicated-task workers; and the swivel-only control is for conference and pull-up use. The one-piece chair has a flexible shell back that responds to the changing postures of people involved in a variety of tasks. The two-piece chair, suited to more dedicated tasks, has a backrest that arches gently in the lumbar region for support and also offers the option of adjustable back height. At the heart of all Basic and Advanced Bulldog chairs is a synchronized tilt mechanism with adjustable tilt tension. All models incorporate 360-degree swivel and either mechanical or pneumatic seat height adjustment. Controls are conveniently located and embossed with graphics depicting how to use them. Seats are extra wide to allow for greater movement.

Discovery®

MANUFACTURER   Fixtures Furniture
Kansas City, Missouri

MATERIALS   Three frame finishes: beige, black or pewter. Over 200 selections from Fixtures Fabric collection. Maharam Synergism textile program, or COM/COL.

Discovery Adjustable and Discovery Economy are meant for multi-task or multi-shift operations. They both feature three easy-to-grip adjustment paddles under the seat with visible graphic instructions to assist multi-shift operators and eliminate the need for operational manuals that often get lost. One paddle controls the pneumatic 5-inch seat height adjustment, a second paddle handles the pneumatic front seat tilt, and the third controls the back inclination. Both chairs have optional independent adjustable arms. Discovery Original is similar to the Adjustable & Economy but also offers three seat widths and five different back heights enabling it to be a task or a management chair. Discovery Passive Plus and Discovery Flair are suitable for general office, management and conference applications. They offer pneumatic height control, knee-tilt, and tension controls which are all operable from a seated position. Discovery Flair is more high styled with a sculptured body and flared arms.

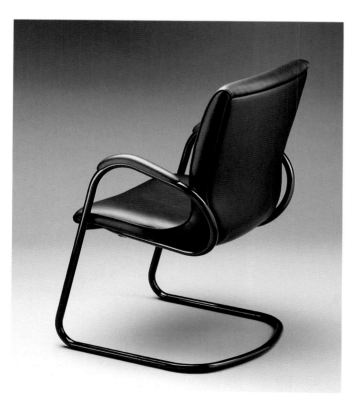

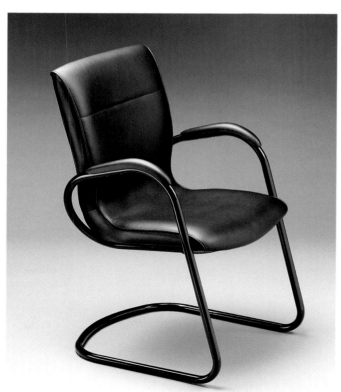

Sulky Collection

DESIGNER   UGGI

MANUFACTURER   Sitag U.S.A. Inc.
Los Angeles, California

MATERIALS   Selection of 30 different Fabric colors or a selection of 35 fine European leathers. COM/COL.

The Sulky Collection includes executive, managerial, and task chairs with pneumatic height adjustment, adjustable seat and back tilt, adjustable lumbar support and height-adjustable arms. They are available with geometrically-shaped back cushions in round, diamond, square, or rectangular formats.

Allegis®

DESIGNER   Babcock and Schmid

MANUFACTURER   Harter
Sturgis, Michigan

MATERIALS   Frame contstructed of high-performance plastic resins. Available in 4 standard finishes. Wide range of standard fabrics and leather. Harter offers a Fabric Enhancement Program with Hendrick, Ben Rose, and Deepa. COM/COL.

Allegis is a passive ergonomic seating system that provides a level of automatic adjustment suitable for clerical, professional and managerial seating. The chair's visual function controls (seat height, seat lock, and back lock) at fingertip level on the chair's front frame provide the user with adjustment instructions for optimum user-adaptation. All models have a seat height adjustment range of 16 to 22.5 inches. Optional locking controls are available for seat and back. Adjustments can be made from a seated postition. The self-adjusting spring tilt mechanism provides automatic adjustment and responsiveness to the user. The seat locks in three positions: forward tilt, upright, and reclining. The chair is available in both large and medium sizes either armless or with two arm styles: loop, and T.

CHAPTER THREE

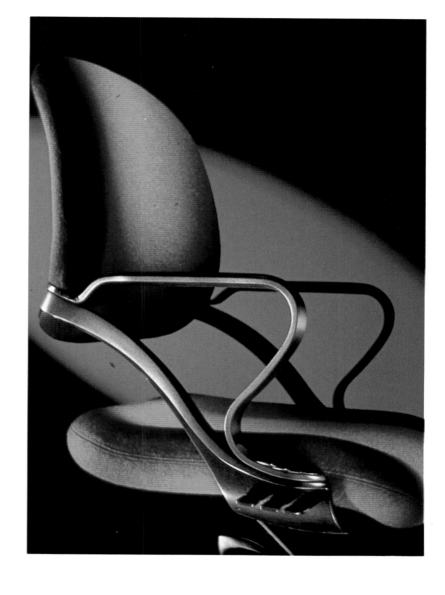

COMPUTER SUPPORT SYSTEMS

Adjustable Workstations, VDT Stands, Keyboard Platforms, Printer Tables

Computer support systems are designed to respond to the performance demands of the technology-intensive environment. These systems are primarily geared to computer-task-dedicated users, but elegant wood versions can also be found in the executive suite. For those who work at a computer for long periods, workstation adjustability can be beneficial to health, comfort, and performance.

Adjustable support stations with single and split work surfaces, for computer monitors and keyboards, are geared to adjust to different heights so an operator's work position can be changed periodically. More sophisticated models also offer work surfaces with tilt mechanisms that angle at varying degrees. This adjustability is an effort to combat repetitive stress injuries and to help alleviate workers' back, neck, or wrist fatigue

that often accompanies intensive computer use. Adjustable-height workstations are ideal for multi-shift situations where different operators use the same computer throughout the day. Height-adjustable surfaces are also especially user-friendly for the disabled. Since the introduction of the Americans with Disabilities Act of 1990, manufacturers report an increase in requests to adapt products to accommodate the special wheelchair height and extra space requirements of the handicapable.

Computer support systems come equipped with varying types of height adjustment including hand cranked, pneumatic, and electrically powered mechanisms. Of course, the electrically adjustable workstations are the easiest to operate, but they are also more expensive. One, with a high price tag, is especially innovative because it can be pro-

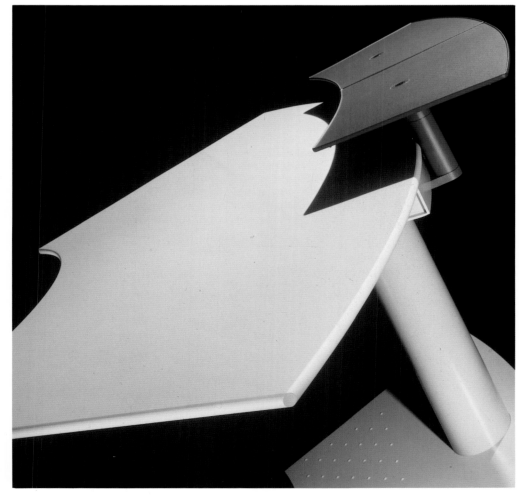

grammed to automatically adjust itself at set intervals throughout the day. In an attempt to meet industry demands for adjustability in the electronic office, a number of manufacturers now have electrically powered workstations in their product line and have incorporated power driven work surfaces into their furniture systems.

To determine the level of adjustability required, it is necessary to assess the intensity of the work performed, or the length of time a worker must spend in certain positions. The best solution is rarely contained in one adjustable component, but is ideally achieved when several adjustable pieces work in concert. According to industry guidelines for adjustability, a worker spending three to five hours per day in a dedicated task position might require such basic supports as an ergonomic chair, a tilt-adjusting monitor, and

a height-adjustable keyboard support. A worker spending five or more hours per day may need the addition of seated-to-standing options, and user work surface adjustability. Accessory items such as foot rests, and wrist or palm supports can also provide an extra measure of comfort to a computer worker's position.

Office workplace adjustability guidelines are designed to inform employers of their responsibility to provide the necessary equipment to help their workers perform efficiently and comfortably. Before selecting the adjustability options, it is important to analyze the work patterns of a company and its employees. Each workplace is unique. Therefore, no one solution can embrace the needs of all. The computer support solutions shown here can help employers meet the adjustability guidelines.

The American National Standards Institute (ANSI) first published guidelines for office furniture suited to video display terminal (VDT) use in 1988. These guidelines, researched and published by The Human Factors Society, Inc., set standards for a worker's physical placement and interaction with computer equipment. The ANSI guidelines address adjustability as it relates to field of vision, seating posture, work surface, monitor/VDT height, and keyboard positioning. Currently there is legislation, based mainly on the ANSI standards, that addresses these adjustability issues. In various locales legislation has already been passed or is still being formulated. The fact is that these guidelines may provide the keys to creating a happier, healthier workplace.

Trakker Adjustable Table

MANUFACTURER   Haworth, Inc.
Holland, Michigan

MATERIALS   Steel structure. All Haworth
finish colors; compatible with Haworth furniture and finishes. Custom shapes and
sizes available.

A split-surface table, the Trakker includes
an optional sequencing function so it can
be programmed to electromechanically
move (from sitting to standing) up to 16
different heights at regularly set intervals.
It "tracks" the time of the user's position.
An entire day's worth of adjustment can be
programmed. When the beeper goes off,
the user pushes the control button to move
the table to the next position. Activated by
a movable control pad, both surfaces are
independently adjustable through a full
16-inch range, from 26 to 42 inches. Four
styles are available: rectangular, inset
rectangular, cockpit, and corner, in widths
ranging from 30 to 72 inches. High-effi-
ciency motors draw power only during
adjustment and should not require additional electrical sources. The table
supports up to 200 pounds on each surface. Tilt is accomplished using a separate
keyboard tilt device.

Sit-stand Height-adjustable Workstation

MANUFACTURER   Steelcase
Grand Rapids, Michigan

MATERIALS   Steel structure with work surfaces that are compatible with Steelcase surface materials.

Electrically driven, the Sit-stand Height-adjustable Workstation offers 25 inches of travel. The keyboard surface adjusts 19 inches, from 23 to 42 inches high. The monitor surface provides additional adjustments, 6 inches above and 5 inches below the keyboard surface. Both surfaces can be adjusted together, and the monitor surface can be adjusted independently. The workstation offers three models with split surfaces: straight, 60 degrees, and a 90-degree corner unit. It supports up to 350 pounds of computer equipment without impacting ease of adjustment, and has an electric drive adjustment with pendant that can be operated from any location on the work surfaces. The workstation is built to withstand frequent adjustment during multi-shift work.

Computer Support Table

MANUFACTURER   Steelcase
Grand Rapids, Michigan

MATERIALS   Steel constructed with work surfaces that are compatible with Steelcase surface materials.

This freestanding split-surface computer support table offers 5 inches of adjustment above and below the monitor surface. Seated adjustment offers 12 inches of travel, and single or monitor surface height range is 23 to 35 inches. Manual crank or electrically powered adjustments are easy to operate. A release lever activates the continuous adjustment range of the keyboard. The table supports up to 100 pounds of computer equipment without impacting ease of adjustment.

VariTask

MANUFACTURER   Mayline Company
Sheboygan, Wisconsin

MATERIALS   Steel constructed base. High-pressure laminate work surface. Unit is available in 20 standard paint and laminate colors, or any specified colors.

The VariTask is a dual-pedestal, fully adjustable work center. A motor actuator independently raises or lowers the work surface and monitor through 15 inches of height adjustment, with a range of 26 to 41 inches on the front pedestal and 27.5 to 42.5 inches on the rear. Tilt adjustability of front and rear pedestals is optional. The VariTask's front surface is available with manual or power tilt, from horizontal to plus 25 degrees. Lifting capacity is 250 pounds with stable support for off-center loads. This product is ideal for computers and heavier monitors, such as CAD, in either dedicated or multi-user environments. The monitor surface runs a generous 18 by 48 inches, and the work surface measures 24 by 48 inches. Two 3-wire grounded electrical outlets are concealed behind the rear pedestal for power access. The VariTask is available in either rectilinear or corner configurations. Single pedestal series work-centers are also available.

Relay High Performance Desk/VDT Table

DESIGNER   Geoff Hollington

MANUFACTURER   Herman Miller
Zeeland, Michigan

MATERIALS   Top and modesty panel finishes are available in a varied selection of laminates, recut wood veneers, and full-cut wood veneers. Painted base finishes complement modesty panels.

This high-performance desk/VDT table is adjustable to support sit/stand work postures. Height adjustment ranges anywhere from 28 to 44 inches. The desk has a 5-degree slope front and a horizontal trough and grommets for cable management. It is made to support surface weight of up to 75 pounds—additional weight will affect ease of adjustment—and has a paddle-controlled, pneumatic adjustment mechanism. The work surface is 30 inches deep by 48 inches wide and accommodates an optional adjustable keyboard tray attachment.

HAWS/Height Adjustable Work Surface

MANUFACTURER   Herman Miller
Zeeland, Michigan

MATERIALS   Steel tracks fit into slotted standards of Ethospace frame or Action Office panel. Work surfaces are available in either of those systems' finishes.

This electrically powered, height-adjustable, single-top work surface has a 20-inch height adjustment range and runs on a track up and down a system's frame or panel. The mechanism, activated by a simple toggle switch, fits Herman Miller's Ethospace and all Action Office systems. It can be ordered separately and retrofitted. The work surface is made to support surface weight up to 150 pounds. Options include: an adjustable keyboard tray, and pull-out auxiliary work surface (breadboard) for a mouse or note-taking. The environment shown is a multi-shift application station.

Satelliti S/60 , S/100

DESIGNER   F&L Design

MANUFACTURER   UNIFOR, Inc.
Long Island City, New York

MATERIALS   Steel columns and bases.
Integral laminate tops in platinum gray.
Video supports and wire baskets in shadow
gray, black, red, blue, and green.

Height-adjustable single-surface workstations are designed to accommodate
complex computer hardware with several
video display units. Monitor support stands
above the work surface have full 180-
degree swivel capability and can be pulled
half across the work surface or pushed
away from it. Rechargeable battery height
adjustment (26.5 to 42 inches) allows user
to sit or stand. Wire baskets provide cable
management. Load capacity is 220
pounds.

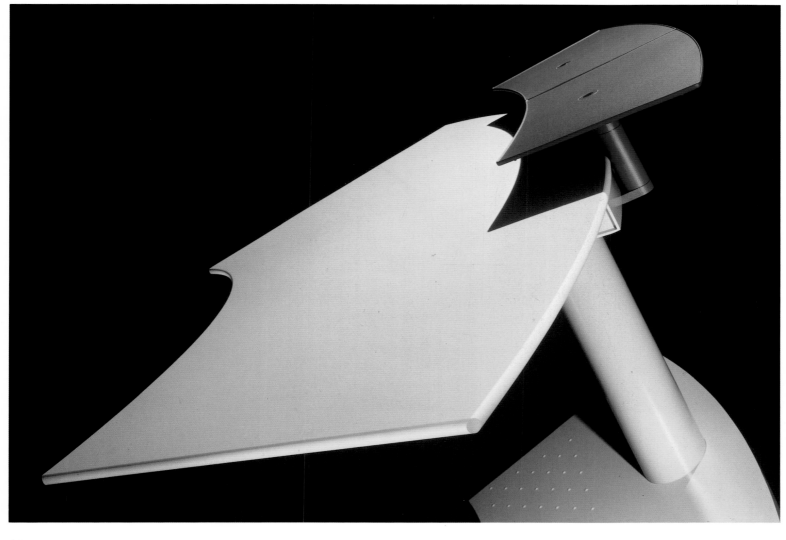

Satelliti S/10, S/11

DESIGNER F&L Design

MANUFACTURER UNIFOR, Inc.
Long Island City, New York

MATERIALS Steel columns, bases, tops, and screens in standard colors: shadow gray, black, red, green, and blue.

Machine support furniture with manual, threaded-column swivel height adjustment is suitable for moderate weight equipment. Full screens with punched holes offer privacy and air circulation. Neutral design appears as an extension of the machine itself and works with almost any furniture line. The S/10 surface adjustment extends from 18 to 23.5 inches and can be sized to the machine it supports. The S/11 has a fixed work surface of 35.5 inches and provides an additional work area beside the computer.

Ergodata Data Table

DESIGNER   Redesigned by Robert La Roche

MANUFACTURER   Precision Mfg. Inc.
Lachine, Quebec, Canada

MATERIALS   Heavy gauge steel structural
members. Work surface: medium density
particle board with plastic laminate in 16
color choices and 9 wood veneer finishes.
Frame available in 5 colors. Custom colors
available.

Data Table's dual-level surfaces with separate hand-crank adjustments for VDT and
keyboard make it especially suited for dedicated terminal users. Available in two
widths, 31.5 and 39.5 inches, the work surface is height adjustable from 16 to 30
inches and tilts plus or minus 11 degrees.
Ergodata options for all units include: privacy panels for individual and linked work
stations; accessory bar; mounted accessories such as task light, letter tray,
telephone pad and paper organizer; overhead shelves and flipper door cabinets;
floor-mounted and mobile pedestals. Extension panels at 8 and 16 inches can turn a
semi-private work area into a private one.

Ergodata Executive Office

MANUFACTURER   Precision Mfg. Inc.
Lachine, Quebec, Canada

MATERIALS   Mahogany veneer with finished black metal components. Other
veneers available.

The 48- by 98-inch primary desk incorporates the usual Ergodata height and tilt
user-adjustable work surface as well as a
height-adjustable productivity extension
top, and right and left conference extension tops. The credenza is created by
mounting a flipper door cabinet onto a
work surface which is user-adjusted for terminal application. A fluorescent task lamp
is mounted below the flipper door cabinet,
and a personal task lamp fits into the
desk-top channel. Freestanding pedestals
fit under work surfaces. All wires and cables are concealed, but accessible within
the communication channels.

Basic Ergodata Work Table

DESIGNER Redesigned by Robert La Roche

MANUFACTURER Precision Mfg. Inc.
Lachine, Quebec, Canada

MATERIALS Heavy gauge steel side cables
and channel. Plastic laminate work surface
in 16 color choices and 9 wood veneer finishes. Steel frame comes in 5 colors.
Custom colors available.

The Basic Ergodata Work Table is a single
surface table equipped with a hand crank
for height and angle adjustments. It features optional VDT platforms with floating
360-degree turntables for sharing data en-
try. Freestanding tables can function on
their own or be linked together to create a
modular desking system. Height adjustment is built into the cables and channels
and is operated by two hand cranks; the
front crank can be fitted on the right or left
side of the tabletop to adjust work surface
height 26 to 30 inches; the back crank angles the surface plus or minus 11 degrees.
A channel at work surface level for easy
access connects the two side cables.
Communication cabling runs through the
channel. Work surfaces measure from 31.5
to 71 inches wide and interaction corner
work surfaces are available in 30-, 45-,
80-, or 90-degree angles. Work surface
depth is expandable by adding a productivity extension measuring 8 or 16 inches
deep. Relocation or reconfiguration of the
system is simple and requires little if any
assembly. Optional cantilevered swivel
arms to support computer terminals are
available.

Disney installation photo by Marius Rooks
Disney Direct Marketing Services, Inc.
The Walt Disney Company Designed by
Engel Picasso Associates, Chatham, New Jersey

8800 Series

MANUFACTURER Steelcase
Grand Rapids, Michigan

MATERIALS Tops and end panels are medium density fiberboard. Tops are finished with a textured, high abrasive, color-coating process available in 6 colors. VDT columns and bases are available in 8 compatible colors.

All the 8800 Series tables and printer stands can be ganged together to form a full workstation. Computer tables in a variety of widths function as stand-alones or integrate into workstation configurations. They are available with or without a hand crank that raises or lowers the height from 26 to 30 inches. Standard cableways and channels provide cable routing and management. Surfaces come 24 or 30 inches deep; 30, 36, 42, 45, 48 and 60 inches wide. Also available with static height adjustment at 26, 28 and 30 inches. Another computer table in the 8800 Series is 30 inches deep and 45, 48 and 60 inches wide with a fixed, keyboard shelf that drops a few inches below the work surface and can be specified to set right or left.

Radius Computer Tables feature a selection of curved table tops that offer ergonomic benefits, such as curved corners to bring reference work closer to the user and allow room for a display terminal at a comfortable distance. The work surface static height is adjustable at 26, 28 and 30 inches.

The adjustable printer stand provides stable, vibration-free support for heavy, high-speed printers or sensitive PCs. It features a wire channel to facilitate cable storage and routing. Work surface static height is adjustable at 26, 28 and 30 inches.

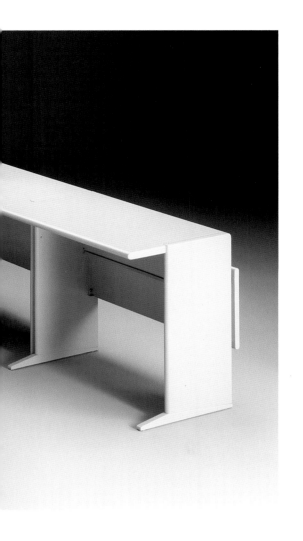

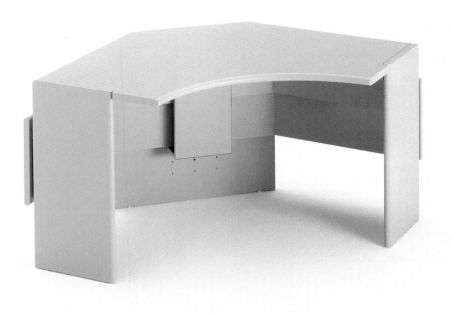

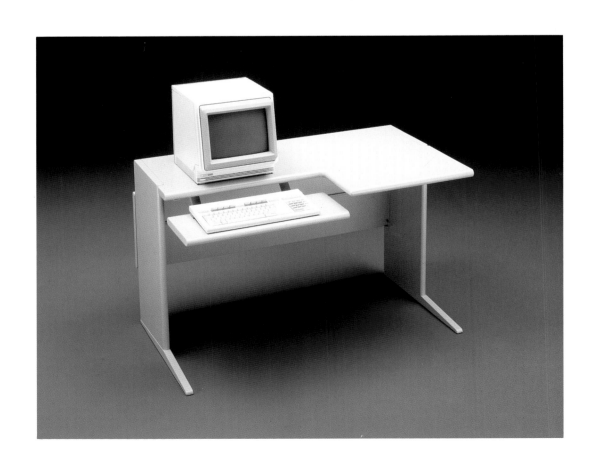

75, 85, 90 Series

MANUFACTURER   Nova
Effingham, Illinois

MATERIALS   The 85 Series is high-pressure laminate in a selection of colors with coordinating work surface nebulas. The 75 Series features radius edge detailing for a more contemporary look. Executive casegoods in the Traditional 90 Series come in mahogany and walnut wood veneer.

Nova's patented collection of computer-integrated casegoods positions the CRT 20 to 30 degrees below the horizontal line of sight—as a result, optimal distance from eyes to screen is easily maintained. The monitor is protected by a tinted, tempered glass window. The out of sight electronic equipment offers an uncluttered work surface with up to 35 percent more space. Placement of the CRT, keyboard, reference materials, and hands—all within peripheral view of the operator—helps productivity. The CRT is adjustable to accommodate various sized computer terminals and provide maximum knee space and ventilation. A Thermoford visor placed on the glass window helps control unusual light situations. An illuminated power switch turns all hardware on/off. The 85 Series can also be used in conjunction with panel systems, freestanding in open areas, or as the nucleus of a private office. Casegoods in the 75, 85 and 90 Series include: desks, returns, credenzas, hutches, and more.

Scooter

DESIGNER Jack Kelley

MANUFACTURER Herman Miller
Zeeland, Michigan

MATERIALS Die-cast aluminum base doubles as a foot rest, and stands on large polyethylene pads that enable it to scoot around easily. Injection molded top. Comes in 3 base and 3 tray colors for a total of 9 combinations.

A computer keyboard support, Scooter also works as a lunch tray, writing desk, telephone stand, projector table, lectern, etc. A foot pedal at the base can pull the tray up to its maximum height of 30 inches; or it can be pushed down to 22 inches and stored under a work surface; a small lever under the front edge adjusts the tilt angle within a 20-degree range. The top has a rounded lip at the front edge to support the keyboard at any one of 4 angles. An optional wire-form document stand attaches to the base of the tray to hold reference papers at a convenient viewing angle. The stand folds down flat for storage.

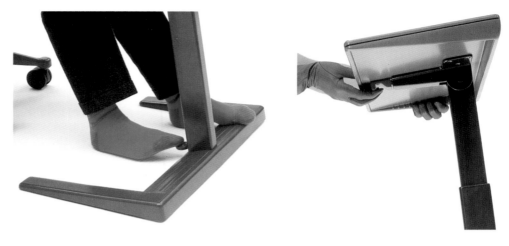

PowerStation

MANUFACTURER   Metamorphosis Design
and Development
Atlanta, Georgia

MATERIALS   Combination die-formed
aluminum and steel frame with electrostatically applied enamel finishes. High-
pressure melamine laminate with radiused
edges on table front and rear. Steel constructed base.

PowerStation is a unique desktop replacement that is easily adaptable to many
workstation environments: it can be used
on PowerBase, its own height-adjustable
pedestal; it can be attached to new or
existing panel systems; or it can be retrofitted onto an existing 60- by 30-inch desk.
PowerStation Corner, designed for panel
systems, is available in three sizes: 42, 45
(to fit Steelcase's Series 9000 furniture
system), and 48 inches.

PowerStation's UserPocket, a U-shaped cut-
out in the WorkLevel, provides support for
the wrists and forearms. The pocket increases functional work space by over 30
percent because the user has more within
arm's reach than with standard desktops.
Other features include: push-button con-
trolled electric motor WorkLevel tilt; monitor platform with optional lift feature; a
PowerBar of six outlets with surge protection; cable management that separates
communication cables from electric wiring;
storage slots; and a flat Reference Level
for phones, books and personal items.

The PowerBase pedestal allows the user to
reposition the PowerStation at the push of
a button to work either seated or standing.

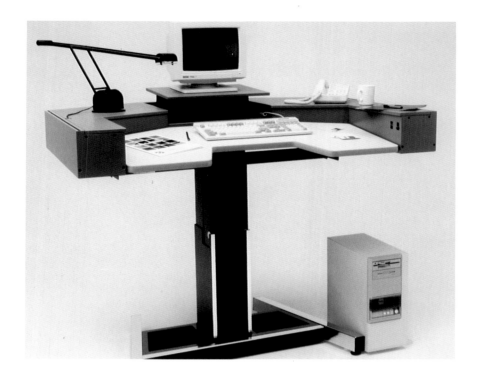

Interaction Tables

MANUFACTURER The Knoll Group
New York, New York

MATERIALS Post-formed plastic laminate, Techgrain, or natural veneer 3-ply work surfaces; formed steel modesty panel and counterweight housing, die-cast feet and extruded aluminum legs in a variety of paint finishes.

Interaction Tables are performance tables featuring: portability, height-adjustability, lay-in wire management, unobstructed kneespace, and sizes and finishes to match Knoll systems, including Morrison Network, Equity and System Z.

The counterbalances table has a fingertip control at either end of the work surface for user-controlled, instantaneous, seated-to-standing height adjustment from 27 to 42 inches high. The mechanism utilizes counterweights, pulleys, and rack-and-pinion guides to counterbalance loads from 0 to 50 pounds on the table. The scope of sizes includes both 24- and 30-inch deep rectangular, and a boomerang-shape, wrap-around surface.

The interaction scope also includes fixed height and manually adjustable tables on glides or casters, in rectangular or curvilinear shapes. Both bases are available with split-top keyboard and mouse surface, offering independent 8-inch adjustment. All tables feature horizontal cable trough and vertical, push-in wire managers in each leg.

Sit/Stand Workstation

MANUFACTURER Tiffany Office Furniture
St. Louis, Missouri

MATERIALS Combination die-formed aluminum and steel frame with electrostatically applied enamel finish. Putty color. Assembly required.

Mobile station height adjusts from seated to standing position (24½ to 38 inches) with the assist of a gas cylinder. The 28-inch-wide keyboard tray has independent height adjustment, can tilt 11 degrees in either direction, and has a 1¼-inch foam pad wrist rest. The monitor tray tilts to reduce glare. A paper holder keeps document in front of operator. The CPU holder at the base of the stand is adjustable. Casters offer mobility, and two are locking. The sit/stand workstation is inexpensive with simple features.

CHAPTER FOUR

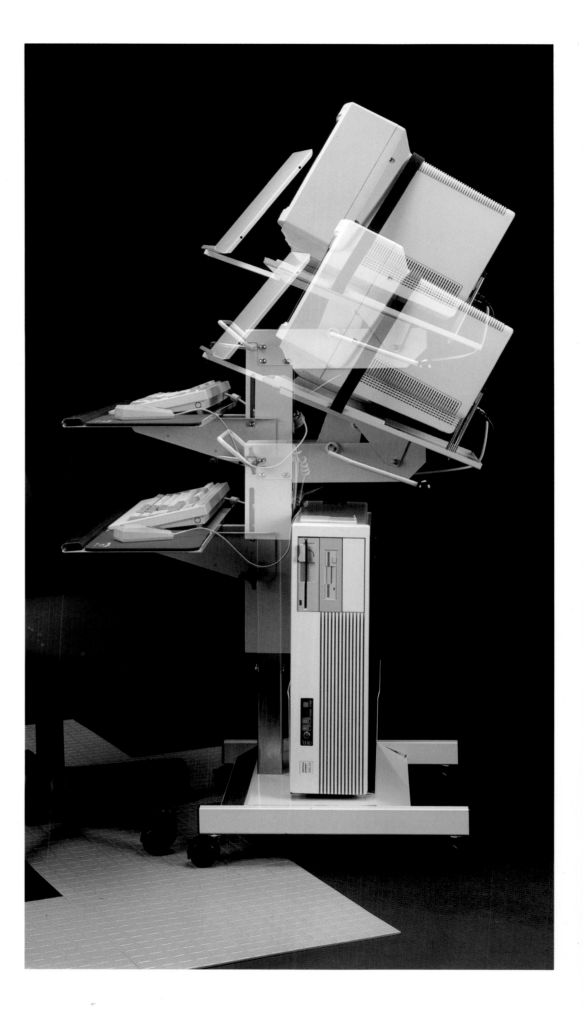

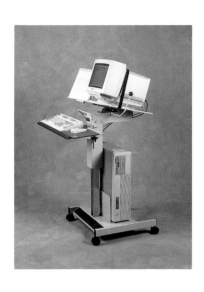

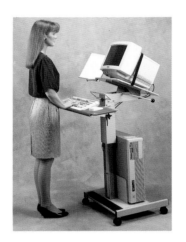

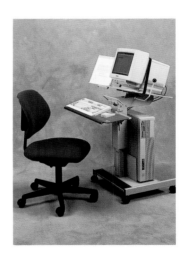

STACKING/GANGING CHAIRS

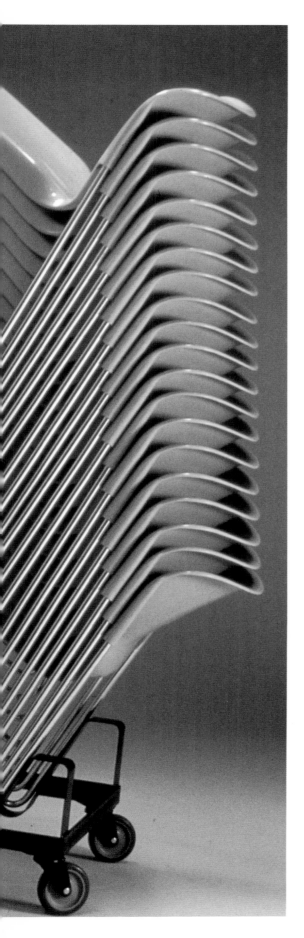

Low, Medium and High Density Chairs

Stacking chairs are the perfect solution wherever occasional, multiple seating is needed. They are referred to as low, medium or high density chairs depending on how many of them can be stacked within a minimum number of feet or inches. Medium to high density chairs are ideal for heavily populated situations such as training rooms, lounges, classrooms, cafeterias, and auditoriums. Lightweight yet durable, they are not only suitable for mass seating but can adapt to multi-situations and part-time needs. Some models allow as many as 40

chairs to be stacked on a dolly and still measure only 4 feet high. It's necessary that a full stack of chairs be within a person's reach for loading and unloading, and the stack measurements must be compatible with standard doorways.

To allow for easy handling during set-ups, rearrangements, and break-downs, medium and high density stacking chairs are light in weight. They are generally constructed of lightweight tubular steel frames with polypropylene seats and backs and weigh only 9

to 18 pounds. Most stacking chairs are also available upholstered, and many even have optional cushioning. For added stability, some models come with a cross brace between the front legs which can be a hindrance to backward leg movement. To address this problem, some chairs have a brace under the seat, whereas others have it built into the overall design. Although stacking chairs come in 4-leg models, most medium and high density stackers have a sled base and offer optional ganging devices for auditorium-style seating and easy row alignment. Other options include tablet arms for convenient note-taking, and racks below the seat for books and other belongings.

Low density upholstered stacking chairs also fill an important niche in the office seating market. These chairs, however, play a somewhat different role than the medium and high stackers. Because they are fully upholstered and more substantial, they stack only five to ten chairs high on the floor or on their own carts. Still, they have enough stature to appear in executive offices as side, guest, and dining chairs.

The Shell chair, designed by Charles and Ray Eames (1950), and the 40/4 high density stacker by David Rowland (1964) are among the earliest stacking chairs. The seating shown here features these, still significant, original chairs of the 50s and 60s, with the best-designed and the most specified stackers of today.

Stacking and ganging chairs account for the second highest percentage of sales in the seating market, after general office chairs.

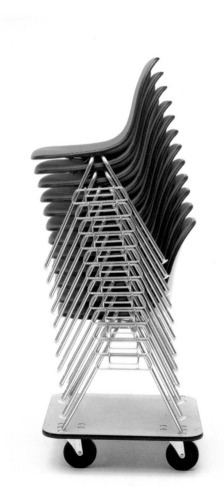

High Density Stacking Chairs

Matrix®

DESIGNER   Thomas A. Tolleson

MANUFACTURER   Krueger International
Green Bay, Wisconsin

MATERIALS   Steel wire frame finished in chrome or electrostatically applied powder-coated epoxy. Curved seats and backrests available in polypropylene colors or wood veneers can also be upholstered in KI fabrics, with or without cushioning, or COM.

As many as 45 side or armchairs, each weighing approximately 17 pounds, can stack within a 79-inch height on the Matrix dolly. Upholstered chairs stack 22 high, cushioned and upholstered 6 high, while veneer models stack only 4 high. The dolly offers easy stacking, transporting and storage. Matrix chairs are available with or without arms. Options include: regular or ganging glides, tablet arms and bookracks.

Max - Stacker & Max-Stacker® II

MANUFACTURER   Steelcase
Grand Rapids, Michigan

MATERIALS   Steel rod frame in 8 colors plus polished chrome. Polypropylene shell in 10 colors. Max-Stacker comes in an upholstered, fabric-wrapped model. Max-Stacker II has optional back and seat cushions. Both are available in selected Steelcase fabrics as well as COM.

Max-Stacker weighs 17 pounds and stacks 40 chairs high within 4 feet on a dolly. Max-Stacker II stacks 35 chairs high on a dolly and also weighs 17 pounds. It is similar to the 20-year-old Max-Stacker but with a different profile: Max-Stacker II has a round back and curved lines. It also provides improved back support and optional cushioning. Other options include a tablet arm, under-the-seat bookrack, and a heavy-duty dolly. Spacer attachments are available to align the chairs.

40/4

DESIGNER   David Rowland

MANUFACTURER   GF Office Furniture
Youngstown, Ohio

MATERIALS   Steel frame finished in
chrome plating as standard. Color-coated
and white outdoor frames also available.
Seat and back: formed metal with rolled-
rim edges, finished with baked-on textured
paint. Optional: molded plywood, or upholstered with foam-covered seats and backs
in a selection of GF upholsteries. Arms:
black plastic as standard, also available in
wood.

The "40 and 4" chair stacks 40 chairs 4
feet high and weighs 16 pounds. Upholstered it stacks 30 chairs 57½ inches
high. Options include regular glides, ganging connectors, dolly, tablet arm, and
bookrack. Smooth tilting action allows the
chairs to be stacked and unstacked quickly
and easily. They may be moved by double,
triple, or quadruple dollies without ganging.

Introduced by GF in 1964, today this chair
is in the permanent collections of several
museums throughout the world, including
the Museum of Modern Art. It is regarded
as the first significant high density stack
chair. St. Paul's Cathedral in London was
set up with fifteen hundred 40/4 chairs to
accommodate the guests for the wedding
of Prince Charles and Princess Diana.

astro®

DESIGNER   David Maslan

MANUFACTURER   Fixtures Furniture
Kansas City, Missouri

MATERIALS   Steel frame, finished in
chrome. Thermoplastic hammock shell.
Seat or back pads available. Specify Maharam Synergism upholstery program,
leather, or COM.

The astro is available in both a sled base
and 4-leg model. The 4-leg side and armchairs stack 20 high on the floor or on the
dolly. Each weighs only 9.4 or 11 pounds
respectively. The sled-base side chair
stacks 20, and the sled armchair stacks 6
on the floor. These chairs are inexpensive,
flexible, and so easy to handle that maintenance people stack them as if they were
throwing a basketball from the foul line.
Neither the sled nor four-leg base is hampered by a cross brace. All are available in
side, arm, and tablet versions. Options include gang glides, bookrack, and dolly.

Ariel™

DESIGNER   David Rowland

MANUFACTURER   Allsteel
Aurora, Illinois

MATERIALS   Carbon steel frame in chrome
or 5 finishes that coordinate with the 11
colors of the injection-molded polypropylene seat and back. Optional
upholstered seats and backs.

Introduced in 1990, Ariel weighs 16½
pounds and stacks 40 chairs (or 20 upholstered) about 63 inches high on its custom
dolly. Options include regular glides, ganging glides for auditorium-style seating, a
field-installable tablet arm, and an under-
the-seat bookrack.

System 12

DESIGNER   Steve Nemeth, Haworth Design Studio

MANUFACTURER   Comforto®, A Haworth Portfolio Company
Holland, Michigan

MATERIALS   Steel rod frame in 4 epoxy paint colors plus chrome. Polypropylene seat and back shell in 9 colors with non-slip, textured finish.

The armless System 12 chair stacks 40 on the dolly within 69 inches and weighs 10.8 pounds (armchair 13.3 pounds). The seat and back are contoured, and a handy grip opening in the backrest top makes the chair easy to transport. A storage cart is also available.

d chair®

DESIGNER   Barry Crone

MANUFACTURER   Fixtures Furniture
Kansas City, Missouri

MATERIALS   Steel rod frame in polished chrome or 5 powder epoxy colors. Lightly textured softone or high-gloss poly-propylene shell. Upholstered version has a molded plywood shell cushioned with poly-urethane foam.

The armless d chair stacks 45 high on the dolly, 12 high on the floor. Each weighs only 12 pounds. Leg clearance is not hampered by a cross brace. It is available in side, arm, and tablet versions. Clear plastic gang glides are optional.

Acton Stacker®

DESIGNER Hugh Acton

MANUFACTURER American Seating
Grand Rapids, Michigan

MATERIALS Reinforced tubular steel
frame comes in chrome or powder-coated
finished colors. Polypropylene seat and back
shells. Cushioned upholstery available in
American Seating's Celebration fabrics program or pre-approved COM.

The Acton Stacker armchair stacks 26 high
on a dolly, 21 high upholstered. It is ideally
suited for seating in offices, and patient or
waiting rooms, as well as cafeterias, training rooms and auditoriums. The open
design under the seat allows for free leg
movement, and the chair's waterfall edge
aids lower leg circulation. The ergonomically sculpted seat and back provides
overall support but is particularly suppor-
tive in the lumbar region. Options include
an armless model, regular and large tablet
arm, bookrack, and connectors for ganging. There is also a tilt-up seat for mass
seating to meet building seating code
requirements.

Attiva™

DESIGNER Jerome Caruso

MANUFACTURER Thonet
Statesville, North Carolina

MATERIALS Steel rod frames available in polished chrome or 15 powder coat colors which complement the shell and arms. Polypropylene shell. Optional partially upholstered seat and/or back.

Attiva side and armchairs stack 30 on a dolly, and between 10 to 12 freestanding. They weigh 15 and 16 pounds respectively. The one-piece shell has linear perforations and rounded edges. Frame and seat flex together reacting subtly to the movements of the body. Options include a stacking tablet arm and bookrack.

Medium Density Stacking Chairs

Perry Seating

DESIGNER   Charles Perry

MANUFACTURER   Krueger International
Green Bay, Wisconsin

MATERIALS   Steel wire frame available in chrome and 5 standard powder-coated colors. Polypropylene seat and backrest in 17 standard colors; upholstered, or upholstered and cushioned in KI standard upholstery, or COM.

Perry Seating provides comfort and passive ergonomics in a medium density stack chair that offers the support of an articulating backrest; the seat is hung from the lower back so that the user's weight counterbalances the tilting pressure of the upper back. Stacking ability is 25 chairs on the transport dolly, and each weighs 17 pounds. They are available with or without arms, and seats and backrests are field replaceable. Options include regular or ganging glides, tablet arms and bookracks.

Parade™

DESIGNER   Rob Scheper

MANUFACTURER   Steelcase
Grand Rapids, Michigan

MATERIALS   Steel rod frame in 8 colors
plus polished chrome. Polypropylene shell
in 13 colors. Optional cushioned upholstery
in selected Steelcase fabrics as well as
COM.

Parade weighs under 18 pounds and stacks
24 on its dolly within 65 inches. It is light
in scale with a frame that juxtaposes arc
and cantilever. The geometric lines and
comfort contoured shell render it appropriate for the masses or the select few.
Options include plastic arm caps, spacer
attachments to align the chairs, plastic or
stainless steel glides, and a dolly.

Nova

DESIGNER Gerd Lange

MANUFACTURER Atelier International
member Steelcase Design Partnership
New York, New York

MATERIALS Steel tubular frame in
chrome, white, or black fusion epoxy. Polypropylene or nylon shell, both available in
custom colors on special contract. Optional
upholstery in a selection of DesignTex Fabrics, Atelier International fabrics and
vinyls, and COM with approval.

Nova's armless model weighs 11 pounds
and stacks 20-25 chairs on its heavy-duty
dolly. Its rounded edges and contoured
seat assure comfort. For added durability,
the steel cross-frame is inserted into the
shell rather than being affixed to it. Nova
is available with or without arms. Options
include seat and back pads, a ganging device, and bookrack. Also available is a
companion piece heavy duty 4-leg stacking
chair.

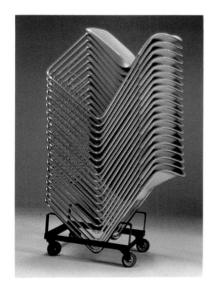

Handkerchief

DESIGNER   Vignelli Associates

MANUFACTURER   The Knoll Group
New York, New York

MATERIALS   Tubular steel wire frame finished in polyester powder or polished chrome. Compressed, molded, contoured seat/back shell of fiberglass-reinforced polyester, integrally colored in black, gray, red or white. Available upholstered in Knoll fabrics, vinyl, leather, and approved COM/COL.

The armless Handkerchief weighs 19 pounds and stacks 25 high on the dolly. The light wire frame and the chair shell give the appearance of a handkerchief floating in space. Options include nylon glides, dolly, and a ganging device for the armless chair. The armchair and the upholstered chairs do not stack.

Concerto

DESIGNER   Alfred Homann

MANUFACTURER   ICF
Orangeburg, New York

MATERIALS   Matte soft plastic shell in
a range of four grays, black, and red.
Chrome-finished frame. Unupholstered,
semi-upholstered (seat and back), and fully-
upholstered in a wide range of fabrics and
leather.

This 4-leg armless chair weighs about 14
pounds and stacks 16 high on the dolly.
The wavy shell of the chair features air
spaces which offer strength and flexibility.
It is also available with arms. A ganging
device and dolly are optional.

Eames® Shell

DESIGNER   Charles & Ray Eames

MANUFACTURER   Herman Miller
Zeeland, Michigan

MATERIALS   Molded, fiberglass-reinforced polyester shell. Steel 4-leg base. Wide selection of colors. Also available upholstered over foam cushioning, in vinyl or selected fabrics. COM/COL.

The armless shell chair stacks 15 high on a single unit dolly within 69¾ inches. Each weighs 10 pounds, or 12 pounds upholstered. A dual unit dolly holds 15 chairs on each side for a total of 30. The armchair does not stack. Options include a tablet-arm chair, ganging device, and two dollies.

The side shell chair won the First National Industrial Designers Institute Award in 1951 and was introduced by Herman Miller in 1952.

148

Jacobsen

DESIGNER Arne Jacobsen

MANUFACTURER ICF
Orangeburg, New York

MATERIALS Shell: molded, laminated
wood veneer in beech, oak, teak, natural
mahogany or maple; stained brown or
black; 16 lacquer colors; fully-upholstered,
or inside seat and back upholstered, or
seat-only upholstered to specification.
Chrome-plated steel legs.

The armless Jacobsen chair stacks 15 high
and weighs under 14 pounds. The armchair
stacks 12 high. Introduced in 1958, this
4-leg chair with a carved wood seat is still
an industry favorite. Options include a
ganging device, tablet arm, and a dolly.
Other versions offer a swivel base with
casters and automatic height adjustor, and
a pedestal base.

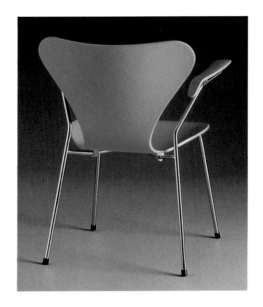

Assisa

DESIGNER Paolo Favaretto

MANUFACTURER Vecta, member Steelcase
Design Partnership
Grand Prairie, Texas

MATERIALS Tubular steel frame with
chrome or black finish. Separate contoured
seat and back of polypropylene with side
ribbing on backrest for added strength.
Matte finish with gloss border in 6 colors.
Arms are tubular steel with polypropylene
armrests. Available with upholstered foam
insets in Vecta fabrics, vinyl, leather, and
approved COM/COL.

Considered a medium density stacking
chair, Assisa stacks 15 armless chairs on
the dolly within 58½ inches and weighs
under 15 pounds. The armchair does not
stack. Options include a ganging device,
black tablet arm with pencil tray, and un-
der-seat wire frame bookrack in chrome or
black.

150

Low Density Stacking Chairs

Versa

MANUFACTURER KI
Green Bay, Wisconsin

MATERIALS Frames available chrome-plated or finished with wear-resistant powder coatings in bright or subtle colors. Nylon arms come in several basic colors to complement frame finishes. Upholstery choices include KI fabrics, vinyl, or COM which can be finished with French seams.

The standard arm and armless 4-leg Versa chair stacks 10 on the floor or on its own dolly. The ganging armchair weighs about 17 pounds; non-ganging about 16 pounds. Both the standard Versa and the full-back model can be specified with a sled base. Armchairs gang with interlocking couplers on the arms, while armless models have couplers at the sides of seats. A tablet arm is available for the standard and full-back 4-leg chair. The conference 4-leg chair stacks 8 on the dolly, is larger in scale with thicker cushions, and the armchair version can be ganged. Transport/storage dolly is optional.

bola®

DESIGNER Ron Kemnitzer

MANUFACTURER Fixtures Furniture
Kansas City, Missouri

MATERIALS Seat and back: upholstered
1-inch urethane foam, contour molded plywood. Frame: 13 epoxy colors or chrome.
Aluminum arms have a molded soft plastic
top insert in all colors. Arms, frame, and
ball glides in mix or match color combinations. Upholstery choices include 176 stock
fabrics, Maharam Synergism Program, or
COM.

The bola side and arm models stack 8 high
on the floor, and each weighs about 16
pounds. A whimsical ball glide, or formal
cap glide, allows the chair to slide easily
on carpeted or hard-surface floors. Its
slightly flared legs make it tip-resistant.
The chair's arched arms offer several comfort zones for sitter's arms. An optional
retractable gang allows the chair to align in
auditorium-type applications, and to work
in dining or office settings.

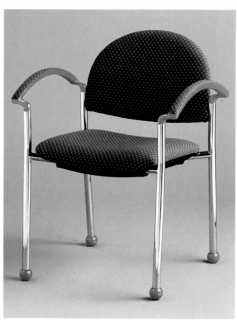

Louis 20

DESIGNER   Philippe Starck

MANUFACTURER   Vitra Seating Inc.
Allentown, Pennsylvania

MATERIALS   Tapered rear legs and shaped
arms are natural aluminum. The body of
the chair is blow-molded polypropylene
which is available in four integral colors:
green, blue, red and gray. Materials can be
recycled since parts are made without ad-
ditives or adhesives.

The Louis 20 arm and side chair stack 8
high and weigh approximately 20 pounds.
A multi-purpose stacking chair, the Louis
20 has unlimited applications including
hospitality, office and home, indoors and
outdoors. The blow-molded polypropylene
body of the chair has mass and volume
without the weight because the process
creates an air-cushion inside. A mix of arm
and armless models can be stacked together giving the chair a unique advantage
in the realm of stackers.

Contura Stacker™

DESIGNER   Robert/Bernard Associates

MANUFACTURER   Gunlocke
Wayland, New York

MATERIALS   Steel frame available in black, brown, or gray. Cushioned with molded foam and fully-upholstered in a selection of Gunlocke fabrics as well as COM.

The Contura Stacker stacks 7 chairs on the floor and weighs 26 pounds. Its oval steel legs and helical incurving arms create a slim profile. The chair has a completely enclosed back. The Contura Stacker can function well in a range of uses, from guest seating to comfortable mass-seating applications. A ganging device and cart are optional.

Proper®

DESIGNER Dragomir Ivicevic

MANUFACTURER Herman Miller
Zeeland, Michigan

MATERIALS Arms and legs are oval steel tubing finished in high-gloss epoxy coating in eggplant, cool tone, or black. Glass-reinforced polypropylene one-piece shell. Upholstery cover, bonded to foam, in a selection of Herman Miller fabrics as well as COM/COL.

Proper is a non-ganging chair that stacks 6 high on the floor within 36¼ inches and weighs 22 pounds. It is an elegant yet practical chair for use in offices, reception areas, dining, or conference rooms. The chair was designed to be viewed from every angle so screws, bolts, and fasteners are hidden by curved metal castings, giving the chair a sculptural quality.

Phoenix

DESIGNER   John Duffy

MANUFACTURER   Gunlocke
Wayland, New York

MATERIALS   Flared-arm frame of steam-bent hardwoods: oak, walnut, maple or cherry. Available in Gunlocke's 20 standard custom finishes. Fully-upholstered: foam filled over webbing, and triple stitched seam detailing in a wide selection of Gunlocke fabrics as well as COM/COL.

The open-arm Phoenix is a non-ganging chair that stacks 5 on the cart and weighs 24 pounds. This enclosed-back chair offers comfort yet is light in scale for modern contract spaces. Phoenix functions in more up-scale conference and dining facilities as well as in offices and public spaces. Other versions include: a larger-scaled chair with open or closed arms, as well as a completely enclosed upholstered chair. A removable wood tablet arm is optional.

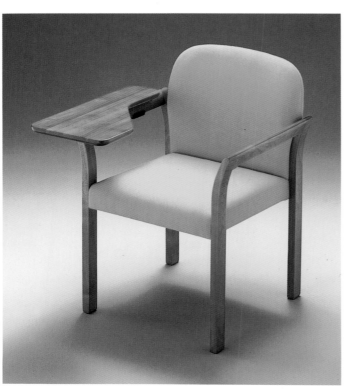

Summa

DESIGNER   Mario Bellini/Dieter Thiel

MANUFACTURER   Vitra Seating Inc.
Allentown, Pennsylvania

MATERIALS   Tubular steel frame. Seat and
back available in beech or black ash veneer,
or upholstered in a full range of Vitra fabrics and leathers. COM/COL.

The Summa armchair stacks 5 high on the
floor within 44 inches and weighs 26½
pounds. It has a free-floating flexible back
and 4-leg base. The chair is a sister to
Onda, the visitor's armchair from Vitra's
Bellini seating collection.

CHAPTER FIVE

MULTI-PURPOSE TABLE SYSTEMS

Conference, Meeting, Training, All-Purpose

To keep up with the changing office environment, tables are expected to be as flexible as the seating and people around them. As the corporate conference room continues to evolve into a more democratic, more dynamic place, the end user must help to define the functions of the space. A large conference table that makes a big design statement is impressive, but it limits the use of the room. A table system with options, however, can help to accommodate a variety of work agendas and a changing roster of participants. Although common rooms are often designed to function as conference,

training, meeting, and break-out areas, modular tables are the elements that provide optimal versatility for such setups. More than ever, for room arrangement flexibility, specifiers are zeroing in on such options as: multi-shaped table components that connect to form a variety of configurations; training tables with wire management capabilities that gang; and lightweight folding tables that store easily.

Overall, furniture manufacturers of office systems and casegoods also make fine coordinating tables to round out their product

lines. The tables featured here, however, are a more selective breed. Most were chosen for their multi-functionalism and innovative design, while others represent significant collections produced by manufacturers of tables only. These "real" table manufacturers, as they like to call themselves, point out that the table business is very customized. These firms carry no substantial inventory but they can provide an incredible variety of sizes, heights, finishes, and colors. Even bullnose edges, always kinder to the elbows, are offered in a wide assortment of colors and finishes to satisfy demands for coordinating or contrasting rims.

Today, specifiers planning office facilities must look at the furniture requirements of the Americans with Disabilities Act of 1990. The law covers accessibility for disabled customers and workers, a measure that could significantly alter a firm's way of doing business. Since the law's provisions go into effect at various times over the next three years, businesses are already surveying ways to comply, and furniture manufacturers are developing suitable products to help customers meet the new regulations. The industry's standard table height is 29 inches, but a table must be at least 31 inches high to accommodate a wheelchair; therefore,

adjustability must be designed into the product. One table manufacturer addresses the problem with a sturdy height-adapter to raise the surface height of its tables for wheelchair clearance. Coincidentally, height-adjustable table desks (see chapter 3) required for dedicated-task workers also answer the needs of the disabled.

Still, for all the talk of adaptability, perhaps the most important detail to look for when specifying a table is adjustable leg glides. The reason, according to one jaded designer, is that no one really notices a table unless it wobbles.

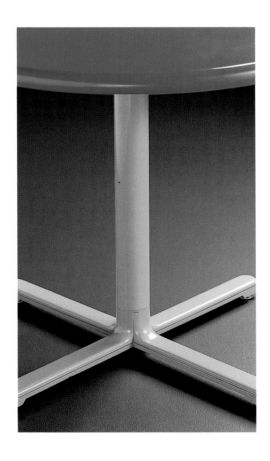

Entropy Tablesystem

MANUFACTURER Lunstead, A Haworth
Portfolio Company
Holland, Michigan

MATERIALS Five standard woods, and 20
finishes. Atop the slab base is a contrasting
inlay of wood or etched metal that slots
flush into the tabletop to create a decora-
tive detail.

Entropy Tablesystem is a modular,
conference/training table system with rectangular, semi-circular, and quarter-round
component tops that join to form a variety
of configurations: U, H, oval, round, and
racetrack. The system is easy to expand
and contract. It is offered with square, soft
bevel, and transitional edge. Custom solutions are readily available.

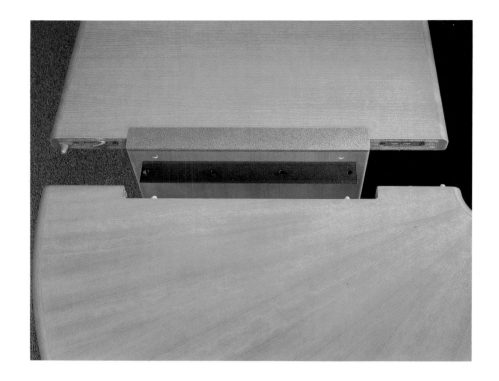

Connect Table Series

DESIGNER Manfred Elzenbeck

MANUFACTURER Davis Furniture
Industries
High Point, North Carolina

MATERIALS Tops available in walnut or
maple veneer, and black or gray plastic
laminate (others can be specified). Wood
screw-in legs and edge rails come in solid
walnut or maple. Metal screw-in legs, edge
rails, and corner elements can be specified
in chrome, black, or gray powder-coat finishes. Interconnecting latches finished in
black.

A mechanical latching mechañism connects one tabletop to another in the
Connect Table Series. The latch mechanism
produces a solid fit that prevents conference table separation. Two people, without
tools, can easily reconfigure this modular
table system. Tables and segmented tops
are available in a variety of sizes and
shapes: square, 32 inches; rectangle and
trapezoid, 64 by 32 inches; and large rectangle, 96 by 32 inches. Reversible tops in
another color can be specified in plastic
laminate only.

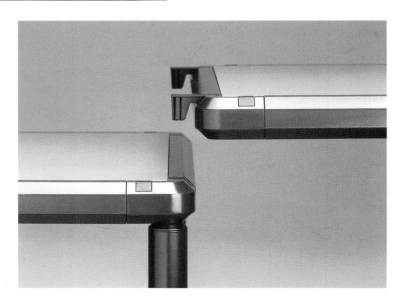

Nexus

DESIGNER Ginbande Design Group

MANUFACTURER Vitra Inc.
Allentown, Pennsylvania

MATERIALS Tabletops: natural beech or black ash veneer with corresponding solid wood edges, or gray laminate with matching ABS edge. Special veneers or laminates readily available. Uniform frame of extruded aluminum. All metal parts in charcoal, or polished chrome. Hard plastic connectors with catch spring.

Nexus is a component-based universal table system with connecting clamps that enable tables and suspension tops to be joined in different formations. The tabletop edge profile permits linkage at all points. Height and leveling adjustment screws are at the top of the leg, rather than the base, for easy access. Tabletop profiles include square, rectangle, and triangle shapes. Tops have bumpers for damage-free stacking. Legs fastened with one bolt make removal for storage easy.

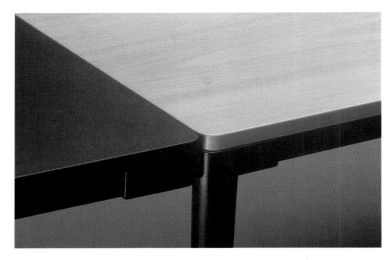

Nexus-T

DESIGNER   Ginbande Design Group

MANUFACTURER   Vitra Inc.
Allentown, Pennsylvania

MATERIALS   Tabletops: natural beech or
black ash veneer with corresponding solid
wood edges, or gray laminate with matching ABS edges. Uniform frame of extruded
aluminum with integrated corner fixing device. All metal parts in charcoal, polished
aluminum or polished chrome. Hard plastic connectors with catch spring.

The Nexus-T tabletop profile is a trapezoid
measuring 60 inches on the long side by
30 inches on all short sides. It has a round
tube leg profile and is 28.5 inches high.

Diffrient Training Table

DESIGNER   Niels Diffrient

MANUFACTURER   Howe Furniture
Trumbull, Connecticut

MATERIALS   Tops: over 27 plastic laminate
colors and 6 wood veneers. Polished Chromax or powder-coated bases.

The Diffrient Training Table, with an optional
wire management trough, effectively handles the inevitable surplus of loose wires in
a computer-based training environment. An
optional, perforated steel modesty panel
flips down to reveal the accessible, yet integrated, trough. Unsightly cables are
channeled through grommets in the tabletop and dropped directly into the full-
length trough which is open at both ends
so that cables can connect to adjacent
tables. Available in stationary, or folding
versions. For efficient storage, the modesty
panel and the collapsible trough fold flat.
Rectangular sizes range from 21½ inches
by 48 inches to 30 inches by 96 inches.
The Diffrient Training Table is part of a
whole collection of tables available in
rounds, squares, and racetracks.

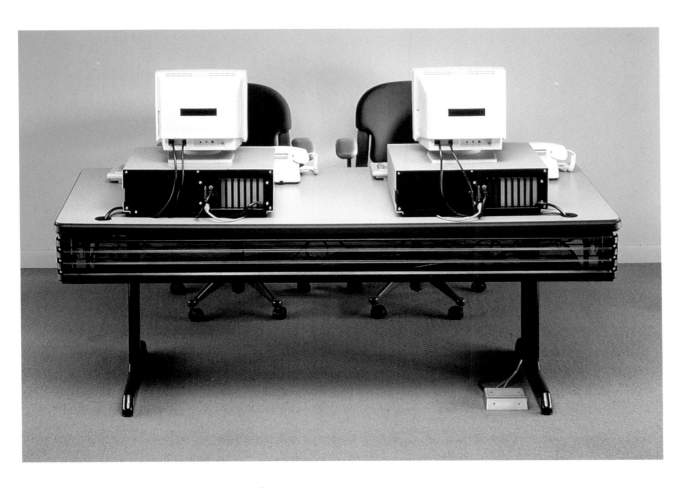

Ballet Training Table

DESIGNER   Douglas Ball

MANUFACTURER   Vecta
Grand Prairie, Texas

MATERIALS   Folding tops: laminate with black ribbed vinyl edge and ABS plastic corner inserts. Fixed tops: plastic laminate, or wood veneer with flat solid wood edge or black vinyl ribbed edge. Base finish: thermoset colors and polished aluminum.

Named for their dancer-like bases that easily open or fold, the X Base and smaller K Base Ballet Training Tables are available in fixed or folding versions. Optional modesty panels have provisions for electrical access and cable management. Modular arrangements can be assembled by using 45-, 60-, or 90-degree connecting tops. Tables have adjustable glides for uneven floors. Available with a mobile storage cart. The series also has round and square tables with 4-prong pedestal bases, and a rectangular tabletop with a non-folding T base.

Spectra II & 500 Series II

MANUFACTURER Howe Furniture
Trumbull, Connecticut

MATERIALS Tabletops are available in a standard selection of wood veneers and plastic laminates. Edges can be wood band, wood bullnose, or vinyl. Legs come in Polished Chromax or 6 epoxy color finishes.

These multi-shaped tables are easily re-configured to accommodate multi-purpose meeting room requirements in a matter of minutes. They provide a budget-conscious solution to the varied needs of all-purpose meeting spaces. Straightforward spring steel clamps efficiently connect the tables into workable configurations for quick change needs. Tables are available in rectangles, squares, rounds, trapezoids, half-rounds and quarter-radius shapes, in a number of sizes. The 500 Series II has square legs, edges, and corners, whereas Spectra II has round legs with radius edges and corners. Both are offered in folding and stationary versions. Optional modesty panels fold out of the way when necessary.

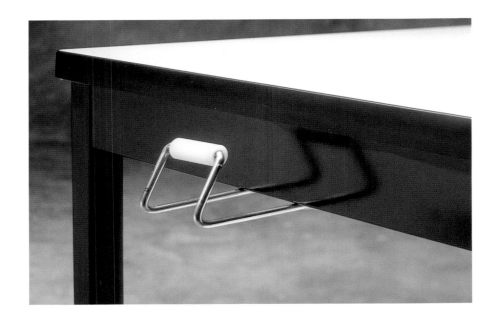

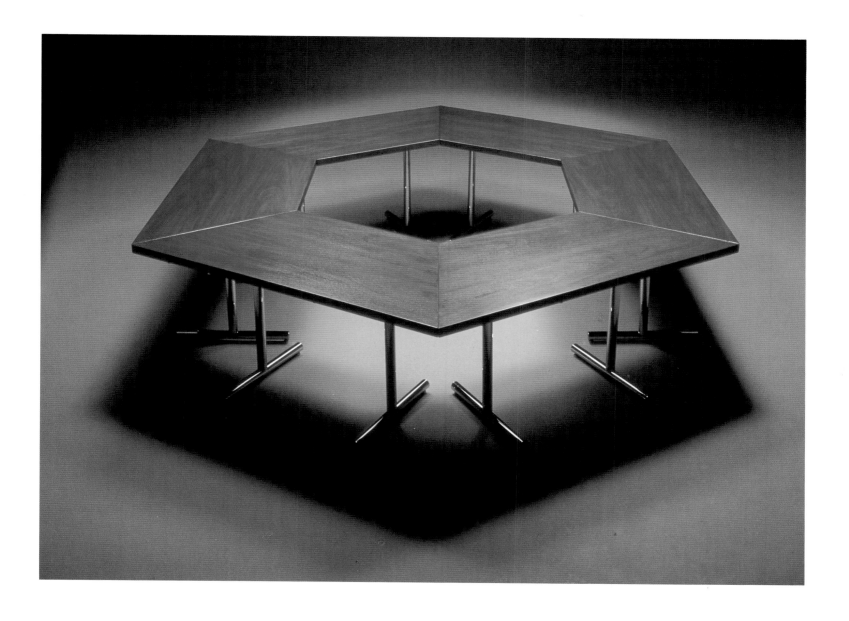

Alliance Table System

MANUFACTURER   Howe Furniture
Trumbull, Connecticut

MATERIALS   Tables and tops are available
in a standard selection of wood veneers and
plastic laminates. Flat, soft vinyl, or hardwood edges. Legs come in Polished
Chromax or 6 epoxy color finishes.

Interchangeable connecting tables and
tops for all types of meeting or training
programs, the Alliance Table System offers
a variety of table sizes that can be ordered
in either folding, flip-top, or stationary versions. The selection includes rectangles,
trapezoids, half-rounds, and crescents;
plus connecting tops in rectangles,
squares, triangles, quarter-rounds and
crescents. All tables and tops feature
Howe's special retractable pull-out hardware for end-to-end, side-to-side, or side-
to-end connections. Simple thumbscrews
make the flush connections possible; no
tools are needed.

Venue Tables

DESIGNER   David Funk

MANUFACTURER   Krueger International
Green Bay, Wisconsin

MATERIALS   Tops: in laminate, 30 selections in wood grains, solids, and speckled finishes; in resin, 20 solid colors, 7 granite colors, and fabric inlays to coordinate with chair upholstery. Also a choice of hardwood veneers. F-style bases have cast aluminum base blades. R-style bases have aluminum flanges and rings which can be accented in colors to contrast with the columns. Other bases available. Steel columns and spiders. Cast aluminum legs, bases and rings.

Venue's F-base tables are available as single or multiple pedestal tables. A reveal in the base blades can be color-contrasted. Tops range in size from 30 to 60 inches in diameter, 30 to 64 inches square, and from 30 by 60 inches to 54 by 144 inches rectangular and racetrack. Venue's R bases come in single pedestals or 4-leg versions. Ring details on the base can be color-contrasted for a design accent.

Stonedge®/Stonecast® Tops

MANUFACTURER   Johnson Industries
Elgin, Illinois

MATERIALS   Stonedge/Stonecast is formed
by mixing liquid acrylic/polyester with various mineral compounds to produce solid
forms or sheets which can be cut and fabri-
cated. Resistant to most stains and acids
and generally repairable on site.

Stonedge/Stonecast is a solid surface material in artificial granite finish which is
molded to the edges of laminate tabletops
without a seam. It is available in 20 matte
colors with a medium hard composition.
Stonecast is the same as Stonedge but it
covers the entire surface of the table. It is
available in ⅛-inch thick sheets that can
be laid up like laminate and post-formed.
Also available, but not shown, are Color-
cast® and Colorflex®. Colorcast no-drip
edge is a seamless polyester resin with a
glossy finish which can be molded to laminate table edges. Colorflex edge is similar
to Colorcast but with a soft composition
and a matte finish.

Tri-color Table

DESIGNER   Jeff Barnes; Barnes Design, Chicago

MANUFACTURER   Johnson Industries Elgin, Illinois

MATERIALS   Wide assortment of custom-colored tops and bases. Tops available in laminate or wood veneer. Numerous edge designs in stained or dyed wood, glossy Colorcast, or matte Colorflex seamless resin. Disc base and column in chrome or brass, or in a selection of baked enamel finishes and colors.

The Tri-color Table with a dyed wood edge and disc base is indicative of the wide range of custom possibilities offered by Johnson. The table shown here was used by a major corporation in its employee dining facility. Available in various finishes, the table can also function as a personal conference table or can be used in break-out rooms for more focused discussions.

Insta-Table

MANUFACTURER Johnson Industries
Elgin, Illinois

MATERIALS Heavy gauge steel.

The Insta-Table system is a mechanism for
attaching a tabletop to a base without the
use of tools. An upper plate comes pre-at-
tached to the tabletop, and a lower plate is
welded to the base column. A positive
locking device allows the top to flip up or
to be completely removed for easy transport or storage. Insta-Table is also
designed to accommodate Johnson's
Height Adapter which snaps into place in 5
seconds and adjusts the table height to
wheelchair clearance. The adapter works
with any Johnson table with the Insta-Table
mechanism.

Folding Tables

MANUFACTURER   Johnson Industries
Elgin, Illinois

MATERIALS   Tops are hexagonal, honey-comb core surrounded by ⅞-inch solid wood frame and enclosed in ⅛-inch two-ply plywood. Top finishes available in laminate or wood veneer. Vinyl, PVC, flat wood edge, wood bullnose, Colorflex edges and more. Enamel powder-coat or chrome steel folding legs.

These lightweight folding tables stand alone or gang to transform multi-purpose rooms in seconds. When not in use they store easily. Weight varies with size, but is approximately 35 percent less than standard solid core construction. Table leg selection includes square, round, high-tech, or bullet-shaped. Options include modesty panels, wire management channel, Quik Lock table latches, and a choice of 4 table carriers.

Mosaico

DESIGNER   Luciano Pagani and Angelo Perversi

MANUFACTURER   Unifor, Inc.
Long Island City, New York

MATERIALS   Tops are high-density composition board with laminate or wood veneer surface. Bases have extruded aluminum legs, a cast aluminum understructure, and a powder-coat epoxy paint finish. Standard laminate in platinum gray, and standard veneers in maple or beech.

Initially designed for a major Milanese newspaper for its editorial work rooms, Mosaico rectangular and trapezoidal ganging tables are ideally suited for meeting and training rooms. The eased-edge top appears to float free from the base structure. Rectangular tables measure 63 by 31½ by 31½ inches. They are designed to gang and offer the maximum number of configurations.

CHAPTER SIX

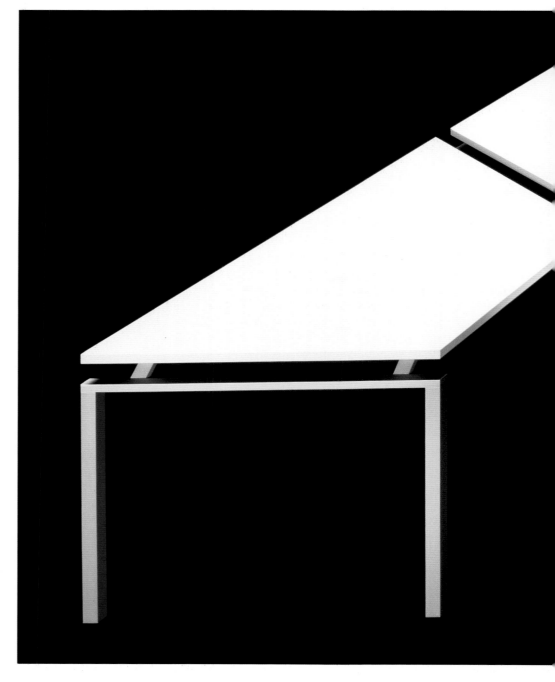

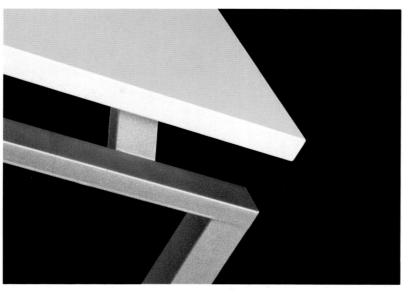

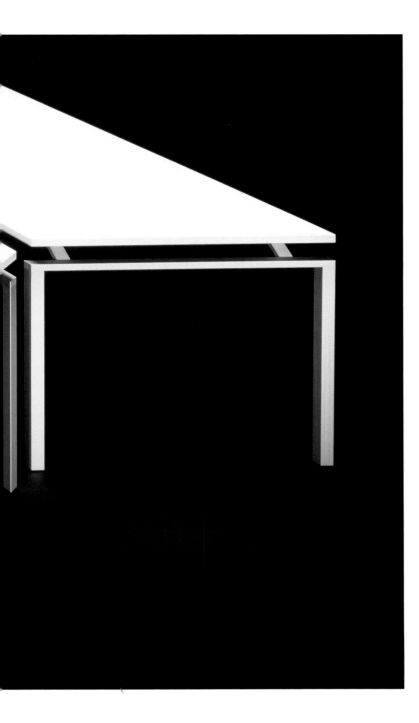

FILING AND STORAGE SYSTEMS

Laterals, Verticals, Overfiles, Pedestals, Cabinets

Storage Systems can provide optimal design solutions for the workplace. They not only serve as storage units, but they can also be used to divide and delineate a space. Their resemblance to over-sized building blocks makes them ideal for creating structures in varied configurations. They can be used to build walls or storage islands, to create credenzas and counters, to divide an open office, to define work areas, or to provide privacy.

Today's filing and storage systems are available in a wide spectrum of colored paint finishes, including metallics and accent colors. Several systems offer optional wood, laminate, and even fabric drawer fronts. Others are available without fronts so that customers can specify their own custom-made designs. One system even has an electronic security device with a digital key pad to protect "sensitive" file records.

Many of the units shown here are compatible with most of the leading systems furniture on the market. In fact, a number of systems

feature their own storage units including lateral files, pedestals, and vertical towers. These units are often so design neutral that they can easily be integrated with other furniture lines to create more individualized work areas.

Storage units are in the process of adapting to the increased acceptance of more personalized workspace in our corporate culture. As workers are permitted to set up their spaces to accommodate the things that make it theirs, storage units are taking on a more personal role. For example, mobile pedestals are now called "personal" pedestals, since their interiors have been reconfigured to hold files as well as more private items.

In yet another corporate phenomenon, the "personal" pedestal has become a movable mini-office. The units are ideal for office workers who operate without a "home base" or who need to move within the office for team projects. One mobile pedestal with a handy pull bar is designed to be carted

around by its owner to whatever office is available. Once the pedestal is opened and the password is keyed into the computer that space becomes the "personal" office for the day. This non-ownership of office is already reflected in a number of corporations where certain areas are designated as "pedestal parking lots."

The "personal" approach in storage systems, however, is just beginning. It has yet to plug into the electronic office with all its wire and cable management requirements, keyboards and computers, faxes and phones. Personal storage systems that integrate a worker's electronic equipment so it can be used and stored in the same unit are already in production.

According to industry studies, the four key factors that specifiers look for when buying files are: price, durability, service, availability (custom capabilities, lead times), and aesthetics.

There are several basic features to consider when evaluating storage systems. Some files are designed as a single case unit with standard drawers; others consist of modular drawers that stack and lock into place. Drawer configurations vary widely and can be selected to meet specific needs. Conventional printed material can be filed front-to-front or side-to-side. Other configurations are available for storage of non-conventional electronic media data such as tapes, micro-fiche, cartridges, disks, and printout paper. Storage accessory options include: center hooks for reels and printouts, T-bars, wire racks, media compartment kits, and trays.

Standard lateral file cabinet drawers are 18 inches deep. For extra capacity, Meridian makes a 20-inch deep lateral file cabinet, and the Knoll Group's Shaw Walker makes a 19-inch deep lateral cabinet. Standard file cabinets have smooth steel surfaces with gloss baked enamel paint finishes. One company produces files with textured (embossed) steel surfaces and a matte paint finish which make them resistant to scratches and fingerprints.

Here are features to consider when purchasing storage systems:

- Drawer suspension, durability of drawer slides influence product life (ask about gauge of steel used, and ball bearing count for smooth operation).

- Case durability, strong case construction to sustain movement when fully loaded.

- Paint finish, type and thickness of application.

- Safety interlock system ensures that only one drawer can be opened at a time, reducing danger of tipping when heavy loaded drawers are fully extended.

- Durable security key locks for sensitive files.

- Sculptured drawer fronts can add a fraction more to the standard 18-inch file cabinet depth.

Stackable Storage System

MANUFACTURER Meridian Incorporated, a division of Herman Miller Spring Lake, Michigan

MATERIALS Heavy gauge steel. Textured, embossed steel surface finish. Non-glare, matte finish that is scratch- and finger-print-resistant. Paint is electrostatically applied baked enamel. Colors include 37 standards that match or are compatible with the panel-systems of leading manufacturers. Drawer front pulls available in inset or outset options in wood or steel. Custom file fronts.

Lateral files: Meridian is the only manufacturer to offer an extra capacity 20-inch deep drawer as well as the standard 18-inch size. These files are unique to the industry because there is no single case, rather its drawers are stackable modules in four heights: 11¾, 13⅛, 15⅛, and 17⅛ inches. Each drawer is a separate unit that stacks and locks into place. The modules can be built to more than 9,220 different heights by stacking combinations of tops, modules and bases. Drawer modules can be reversed, and overheads and pass-throughs incorporated where necessary. There are five bases, from 1 to 4½ inches, and four tops including a 6½-inch H planter top.

189

Meridian's vertical files embody all the qualities of their lateral files. Letter and legal widths come either 22 or 28 inches deep. Pedestals in letter or legal widths, and depths of 18, 22 and 28 inches can be system suspended or freestanding, fixed or mobile. Suspended pedestals are compatible with most major manufacturers' systems. Freestanding pedestals fit under most work surfaces, can be specified to meet counter heights, and have concealed casters.

Media/storage cases (cabinets) coordinate with laterals, verticals, and pedestals. They have removable/adjustable shelves for varied software and computer peripherals; coat rod and shelf combinations; and hanging bars to hold computer or letter paper and all size computer reels. Cases are available in four standard heights, from 29 to 69 inches, and two widths, 30 and 36 inches.

Electronic Locking Files

MANUFACTURER   Meridian Incorporated,
a division of Herman Miller
Spring Lake, Michigan

MATERIALS   The same as Meridian's standard files, to assure uniformity for offices
that require both types of files.

For security of filed materials, this system
throws away the conventional key lock and
employs an electronic key pad locking device—activated by punching in a 5-digit
code. The code is changeable in minutes,
and there are 7,776 locking combinations.
Access codes can be programmed to open
specific drawers within each file for a high
level of security. Electronic Locking Files
provide document security for up to 6
drawers. An additional security option is a
readily adaptable computer software package that integrates the system with desk-
top PCs. A hand-held rechargeable power
supply is available in the event of a power
failure.

Wood-Front Files

MANUFACTURER Meridian Incorporated, a division of Herman Miller
Spring Lake, Michigan

MATERIALS Heavy gauge steel. Tops and drawer fronts may be specified in light grain recut wood veneer finishes, or light ash, mahogany, mahogany dark and inner tone. Veneers are sealed to resist surface mars. The 44 matte paint finishes complement the choice of woods for fronts and tops.

Wood-Front Files are an addition to Meridian's Stackable Storage System. The line integrates steel structured file units with wood fronts available in fine wood veneers in a range of architectural designs. Chamfered wood-over-metal drawer pulls are available in left, right, full-width, and centered configurations. The file modules can be stacked and reversed in freestanding or room-divider configurations. There are three widths: 30, 36, and 42 inches; drawers come in two heights: 11¾ and 13⅛ inches; and two depths: 18 inches, and Meridian's extra capacity 20-inch depth.

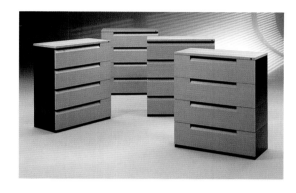

800 and 900 Series Lateral Files

MANUFACTURER Steelcase
Grand Rapids, Michigan

MATERIALS Heavy gauge steel. Smooth surface finish. Available in over 50 paint colors. Wide range of solid and textured paint colors plus laminate, wood, and fabric selections. Customiz Program offers any choice of paint, wood stain or fabric colors. PerfectMatch duplicates any color choice. Fabric-covered, back or side, hang-on acoustical panels for all 64¾-inch-high lateral files. Tops in two styles: self-edge (square) in wood or laminate; bullnose in laminate only. Tops can be used on a single file or on several.

Standard lateral files have 12-inch-high drawers and shelves. They are available in three widths: 30, 36, and 42 inches; five heights with 2 to 5 drawers; and 18 inches deep. There's a choice of drawer and shelf interiors, including compressors, hanging folder frames, dividers and rails. There are top drawer pulls, and bottom receding door pulls. All 4- and 5-drawer-high files are available with a pull out posting shelf. Buildup Lateral Files fill basic cabinets with any combination of drawers and shelves in heights of 3, 6, 9, 12, and 15 inches, with the exception of the 900 Series which has no 3-inch-high drawers.

Optional fixed shelves are available with and without doors. The 12- and 15-inch-high fixed shelves come with receding doors, and the 12-inch also comes with a sliding door. Electronic media storage components are available. Storage walls can be created using storage cabinets, over-files and lateral files, all of which are dimensionally compatible and designed for modularity. Overfile widths correspond to lateral files and are available in one- and two-shelf models with dividers and locks. File and cabinet bases come in open leg or enclosed box with snap-off fronts for wiring access.

730 and 970 Series Storage Cabinets

MANUFACTURER Steelcase
Grand Rapids, Michigan

MATERIALS Heavy gauge steel. Smooth surface finish. Available in over 50 paint colors. Wide range of solid and textured paint colors plus laminate, wood, and fabric selections. Steelcase's Customiz Program and PerfectMatch.

Cabinets are available in four heights, from 41¼ to 80½ inches; one width, 36 inches; and two depths, 18 and 24 inches. Series 730 has recessed rectangular door pulls that match 800 Series lateral file pulls. Series 970 has full-length integral door pulls that complement the 900 Series lateral files' full-width pulls. Supply cabinets offer snap-in shelves adjustable on 2-inch centers, or centerhooks to hang reels and printouts. Wardrobes are the same basic cabinet with the shelves removed and the addition of a coat rod. Combination wardrobe/storage cabinets can be ordered with a coat rod on one side, and adjustable half-shelves on the other. A full-width shelf is optional.

Calibre Files and Storage

MANUFACTURER   The Knoll Group
New York, New York

MATERIALS   Heavy gauge steel. Smooth
surface finish. Available in over 38 paint
finishes and a broad selection of metallics
and accent colors. Optional wood or laminate drawer fronts to complement The
Knoll Group's Reff System 6 or Morrison
Network. Custom colors at no upcharge.
Custom file fronts.

Calibre lateral files can be used with Knoll
Group and other systems as well as in freestanding applications. Features include
radiused drawer pulls and a seamless,
single-piece outer case. All units are 18
inches deep and 2 to 5 drawers high with
12-inch drawer combinations.

In addition to standard 12-inch drawers,
openings are available in five heights: 3,
6, 9, 12, and 15 inches. Four case widths:
30, 34, 36, and 42 inches can be specified in standard configurations with a
variety of drawers, fixed shelves, roll-out
shelves with receding drawers, or a 3-inch
posting shelf. The unique 34-inch-wide
units can be wrapped by a centerline modular panel system. A unique interlock
mechanism engages the rear center of the
drawer to prevent leveraged access at either side of the drawer. Calibre's double-
wall case construction allows fully-loaded
cabinets to be moved without damage to
the unit. Base heights are available to
match furniture heights. Storage/Wardrobe
cabinets in corresponding heights with
hinged doors or open shelves are 30 and
36 inches wide. Cabinets can be ordered
with a coat rod on one side, and adjustable
half-shelves on the other. Armoire is a single storage unit that combines lateral files
with an overfile, available in heights of 12,
24, 36 and 48 inches.

Multistor

MANUFACTURER Kimball
Jasper, Indiana

MATERIALS Heavy gauge steel. Available in 21 standard colors. Black finish is standard on all interior drawers, shelves, exposed hardware, hang file bars, dividers and media frames.

Lateral files are available in five case heights, 2 to 6 drawers high; three cabinet widths, 30, 36, and 42 inches, and 18 inches deep. Five drawer sizes range from 3 to 15 inches and feature full-width pulls. Multistor offers an overfile (23⅞ inches), and storage and wardrobe cabinets with hinged doors. Lift-up doors can be fitted with pull-out or fixed shelves. The MultiTray organizer has three vertical chambers slotted for shelves and tray inserts that form 129 individual compartments. Storage cabinets are available in corresponding heights with hinged or sliding doors, with or without shelves.

Wardrobes are hinged door cabinets with a selection of storage accessories including coat rods, paper trays, and shelves. Combination wardrobe/storage cabinets can be ordered with a coat rod on one side, and adjustable half-shelves on the other. Modular filing, drawers, doors, internal components, and the interlock and locking systems are all designed to be easily field reconfigured.

198

LF, LFF Lateral File Series & EDP Storage Cabinets

MANUFACTURER   Harpers, a subsidiary of
Kimball International Company
Torrance, California

MATERIALS   Heavy gauge steel box formed
on all four sides. Available in over 30 standard paint colors.

Lateral files feature flush handles or full
pull drawer fronts. They are available in
four case heights ranging from 2 to 5
drawers high, and in three cabinet widths:
30, 36, and 42 inches, and 18 inches
deep. The 5-drawer-high lateral files have
an optional lift door with a pull-out shelf in
the top position which increases the overall height by one inch. Any lateral file
drawer may be replaced by two half-height
drawers. Drawers are removable and interchangeable without the use of tools and
are equipped with a patent pending security Interlock System. Overfile units come
in 30-, 36-, and 42-inch widths and are
29½ inches high. EDP (Electronic Data Processing) Storage Cabinets are available in
30- and 36-inch widths in heights to match
lateral files. Shelves accommodate hanging EDP channels, Wilson Jones System of
electronic media storage. Cabinets come
with hinged doors, and with or without
shelves.

Radius Profile Series

MANUFACTURER   Office Specialty—Storwal
Holland Landing, Ontario, Canada

MATERIALS   Heavy gauge steel. Available
in 40 standard colors or custom colors at
no upcharge except for special whites and
metallics. Two-tone combinations at slight
upcharge. All radius fronts can be upholstered in COM fabrics, leather, or vinyl wall
coverings.

Lateral files feature soft radius edge detail
across each drawer and recessed side
pulls. Available in 41 standard case
heights and two widths, 30 and 36 inches,
they come 2 to 6 drawers high and are
18⅝ inches deep. Drawers can also be
combined with hinged door options. Fixed
front drawers or lift-up receding doors, with
pull-out or fixed shelves are available. Cabinets with hinged doors are 30 and 36
inches wide in heights corresponding to
lateral files. Options include slotted
shelves, dividers and coat rods.

The Workplace Locker is a personal storage
cabinet suitable for workstations and private offices. One side functions as a
typical ventilated sports locker, and the
other side provides modular storage for
business or personal items.

Radius Pedestal Series works with Radius
lateral files to create desks and credenzas.
Pedestals feature seamless, wrap-around
cases and flush side pulls for a clean look.
They are available 18, 22, and 28 inches
deep and can be specified as floor standing or mobile with the addition of
concealed casters.

Custom Profile Series is an edition of files,
cabinets and pedestals without drawer
fronts ready to be custom matched by the
user. Schematic "shop drawings" are in the
product price list. Custom allows for simple
field or shop installation and provides maximum freedom in material selection.

Radius Profile
Impressions

MANUFACTURER   Office Specialty—Storwal
Holland Landing, Ontario, Canada

MATERIALS   Heavy gauge steel with extra
painted metal liner in drawer front. Refer
to Radius Profile for finish and color
details.

A design addition to the Radius Profile
Series, Impressions offers the option of
creating geometric symbols, logos, or patterns in the drawers or doors of metal filing
units. Metal file front features a design
cut-out and a metal liner in a contrasting
color behind it to create a 3-D impression
of the custom design.

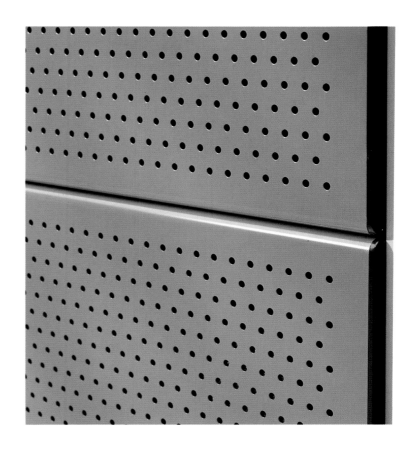

Radius Profile Acoustical File

MANUFACTURER Office Specialty—Storwal
Holland Landing, Ontario, Canada

MATERIALS Heavy gauge steel with foam
insert liner in drawer front. Refer to Radius
Profile Series for color details.

This acoustical addition to the Radius Series has perforated drawer fronts and liners
so that airborne sound passes into the
cabinet. Sound is absorbed by the cabinet
fronts and the paper filed inside. NRC rat-
ing of .95.

Storage Centers

MANUFACTURER Office Specialty—Storwal Holland Landing, Ontario, Canada

MATERIALS Heavy gauge steel. Smooth surface finish. Available in 40 standard colors or custom colors at no upcharge except for special whites and metallics. Two-tone combinations at slight upcharge.

Storage Centers utilizes a 1½-inch module to offer increased flexibility within the entire product range. The system has a total of 41 case heights, from 17⅝ to 79⅜ inches, three widths, 30, 36, and 42 inches, and is 18 inches deep. Files have full-width drawer pulls. The line includes lateral files, overfiles, and storage and wardrobe cabinets with hinged or sliding doors. Cabinets can be custom configured using drawer heights ranging from 3 to 16½ inches. The most popular sizes are preconfigured as standards for convenience.

Storage Centers is similar to the Radius Profile Series but has the additional 42-inch-wide overfiles that range in height from 17⅝ to 32⅞ inches, and more interior options.

Puppy

MANUFACTURER Herman Miller Zeeland, Michigan

MATERIALS Case finishes: 6 laminates; 4 recut wood veneers; 3 full-cut veneers. Metal handles on 2 sides for easy pulling.

A mobile, lockable personal storage cart with a handy pull bar, Puppy has a top that slides off to one side for a knee-height reference surface. A shallow organizing tray slides off to the other side for easy access to hanging files inside. It measures: 15⅛ by 18¾ by 23⅞ inches high. A drawer insert is included. The file drawer includes two file converters to allow side-to-side filing of all standard-size papers. The Puppy is a freestanding piece from Herman Miller's Relay system.

Lateral Files and Storage System

MANUFACTURER   Haworth
Holland, Michigan

MATERIALS   Heavy gauge steel. Files in 22 paint finishes. Fronts available in 13 wood finishes. Tops available in steel, laminate, and wood veneers. Custom Colors.

Haworth's lateral files have radiused corners. The system includes 2- to 5-drawer files in a range of 4 heights, from 26⅞ to 62¾ inches. File widths are 30, 36 and 42 inches, and they are 18 inches deep. Drawers are available in heights of 3, 6, 9, 12 and 15 inches with pulls that are integral or full length. Receding doors with roll-out shelves are also offered in all drawer heights. The two-drawer credenza is height compatible with desk and system work surfaces. Custom drawer configurations are offered. Wardrobe/storage cabinets with hinged doors are 30, 36, and 42 inches wide and are available in heights to match 5-drawer lateral files. The storage cabinets come in 3 heights including 38⅞ inches. Both shelves and coat rods can be adjusted up or down in increments of 2¼ inches. Bookcases, 36 inches wide, come in 2-, 3-, 4-, and 5-high units, and are equivalent in height to lateral files, storage cabinets, and the credenza file. Overfiles provide additional storage on top of any height lateral file, wardrobe or storage cabinet. Available 29¾ inches high with two full-height sliding doors or open shelf. The files and storage units are compatible with Haworth's complete line of freestanding steel furniture, but can fit within any office furniture environment.

Lateral Files and Cabinets

MANUFACTURER   Allsteel
Aurora, Illinois

MATERIALS   Heavy gauge steel. Spectra-One palette of over 40 standard colors, plus custom colors at no upcharge for 11 or more units. Four pull styles: full-width in light oak or mahogany; full-width in vinyl-clad steel; contemporary recessed mirrored chrome; and rectilinear integral pull. Tops are available in self-edge or radius-edge laminates, and in wood veneers.

Allsteel's standard lateral files are conventional rectilinear case files in three widths; 30, 36 and 42 inches; and eight heights from 26¼ to 76¾ inches with 2 to 6 drawers, and they are 18 inches deep. There's a choice of drawer and shelf interiors, including compressors, hanging folder frames, dividers and rails. Files are fully adjustable to accommodate letter, A 4, legal and EDP (electronic data processing) filing.

Buildup lateral files fill basic cabinets with any combination of drawers and shelves in heights of 3, 6, 9, 12 and 15 inches. Case heights range from 26¼ to 76¾ inches. Fixed shelves with and without doors are optional, and add-on bases are also available.

Storage cabinets, overfiles, and lateral files are dimensionally compatible and designed for modularity. Overfile widths correspond to lateral files and are 16¼ and 27¾ inches high. Storage cabinets, available in a range of four heights from 39¾ to 64¾ inches and widths of 18, 30 and 36 inches, are meant for housing computer media, wardrobe and miscellany.

Allsteel offers a line of lateral files which complements its latest AURORA office system. The files echo AURORA's soft radiused-edge components and are available in 4 heights, 3 widths and 8 colors with optional wood veneer fronts in 9 finishes. Allsteel also offers the Options LF custom front lateral file program.

Storage Walls and Partitions

MANUFACTURER VOKO
Pittsburgh, Pennsylvania

MATERIALS Heavy gauge steel. Smooth surface finish. Wide palette of standard colors. Laminate and veneer.

Because this European system is based on metric modules it can be difficult to specify. Therefore, the client gives space dimensions, and the factory in Germany specifies the necessary parts and pieces. The system is versatile and can be used against the wall, freestanding, or floor-to-ceiling with a finished back and a finished top. The internal arrangement of the cabinets can accommodate the varied demands of organizing and filing. Internal fittings include standards such as suspended and lateral filing, shelves, general storage, wardrobe cupboards, personal lockers, and display and bookcase units with sliding glass doors. The system's more unique interiors include kitchen and bar units, safes, and a flip-out bed.

VOKO also offers a partition system which features recessed, slotted steel tracks that can be fitted into the vertical joints to suspend components. The design of the partitions makes it possible to hang shelves and flipper-door storage units on a concealed tracking system.

Moduline is a visual aids system that fits the VOKO partitions. It consists of a continuous aluminum rail which mounts onto the partitions and holds flip charts, whiteboards, and shelves.

CHAPTER SEVEN

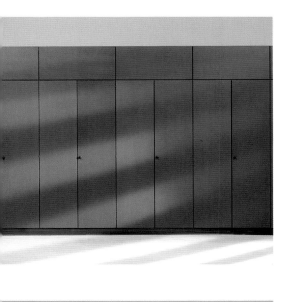

ACCESSORIES AND LIGHTING

Computer Support Tools, Paper Management Systems, Visual Aids, Task Lighting

Accessories for the office have become a serious business. These "tools of the trade" have always facilitated or organized the work flow, but now they are meeting new challenges by providing healthier, more comfortable solutions for the electronic office. We are learning the very human price of technology: chronic headaches, neck and back strain, carpal tunnel syndrome, and a host of other assorted aches and pains. Accessories are addressing these health concerns with products that are designed to reduce stress, strain, and pain. Computer support accessories and organizational tools can surely help to create a more productive and comfortable work environment.

Computer Support Tools

Foot rests continue to enter the workplace at a stepped up pace. Combined with an ergonomically designed chair and adjustable

work surfaces, they can help improve the user's posture and release tension. According to some of the VDT legislation they "shall be provided upon the request of the operator." Although sales indicate workers want them, some ergonomic experts claim that foot rests support a limited area and may, therefore, restrict an operator's mobility within a workstation. Nothing beats placing the feet flat on the floor, they advise. Nonetheless, it seems that some foot rest users like them so much that they have asked manufacturers to add heating elements and foot massagers.

Wrist rests (a.k.a. palm rests) should elevate and align the wrist to the computer keyboard and provide a comfortable surface for resting the wrist in a neutral posture when retracting from keying. The proper rests are said to decrease the potential for nerve irritation and, like the foot rests, "shall be provided upon request of the operator." Wrist

rests are available with height and angle adjustments, and with a nylon covering for easy cleaning.

Adjustable keyboard supports provide a supplementary surface and ease height and placement adjustment. They are ideal to help users work more effectively and comfortably with their equipment. It is important to make sure that the keyboard tray doesn't eat into the user's leg room.

Paper Management Systems

Rail systems are designed to handle paper and clear work surfaces. Mounted on furniture system panels, they are hung with an array of organizing components. In freeing up work surfaces they offer another level of humanization in the workplace by customizing the work environment. The systems are generally available in a wide selection of colors to coordinate with furniture systems.

Visual Aids

Visual boards and modular tracking systems can facilitate presentation and training methods in the meeting and conference room, or the executive office. Visual boards with framed porcelain writing surfaces and marker-board pens are the media for conveying the message. The boards also come in handsome cabinets of wood or laminate, with face doors that open to reveal tackboard panels on each door and an optional projection screen.

Tracking systems are linear rails that mount to the wall and hold presentation components that can be configured and reconfigured to suit a broad range of communication requirements.

Lighting

Offices used to have 2- by 4-foot fluorescent lighting throughout the ceiling flooding the entire space. Today offices are more efficient with low-level lighting in the corridors, high levels where necessary, and adjustable task lights for lighting exactly where it is needed.

These lights are ideal for providing illumination of the individual work area for a particular task and can function freestanding on a base or mounted on a furniture system panel or rail. Most furniture systems offer task lighting—in the form of fluorescent tubes with diffusers—under the overhead cabinets, but task fixtures can also help personalize the workspace since many are handsome enough to give an aesthetic lift to the environment.

There are three important considerations to take into account when purchasing lighting: energy efficiency; color quality of the light source (it should be consistent throughout the office); and cost. Several types of lamp sources are available. Compact fluorescent is energy efficient and offers three different color temperatures: cool white, daylight or warm white, and warm pink. Halogen is a more technically advanced form of incandescent lamp that gives a high color quality of light. It is not as energy efficient as fluorescent lighting and tends to run hot. Incandescent is the least energy and cost efficient with a quality of light that is not as pleasing as halogen or fluorescent.

Indirect or uplighting is the ideal light source because it is glare-free and gives an overall glow. Within the last several years lighting designers have devised panel-mounted uplighting for furniture systems. This glare-free illumination can make a significant contribution to worker productivity and comfort in VDT-dominated facilities.

The rising incidence and growing awareness of cumulative trauma disorders in the workplace has generated important industry standards and has compelled accessory and lighting manufacturers to respond with products designed to reduce such work-related risks. The American National Standard for Human Factors Engineering of Visual Display Terminal workstations (ANSI/HFSVDT Standard No. 100-1988) pro-

vides guidelines for workstation seating. "Arm rests, wrist rests, and foot rests shall be provided upon the request of the operator. Wrist rests shall enable the operator to maintain a neutral position of the wrist while at the keyboard, and shall be padded and without sharp edges."

States and municipalities throughout the country are currently generating legislation to establish local standards for lighting the workplace. For example, San Francisco's VDT Law requires that workstations must be illuminated with lights arranged to avoid visual glare and discomfort. The illumination level has to be within 200-500 lux, and task lighting must be made available upon the request of the VDT operator.

Foot Rest

MANUFACTURER Details, member
Steelcase Design Partnership
New York, New York

MATERIALS Counter-pressure foamed
styrene, steel, and vinyl. Two colors: chalk
and meteorite.

Foot Rest offers four height adjustments
from 3 to 6 inches above the floor. Its
curved surface provides variable angle
positions. The platform is approximately
16 inches wide by 12 inches deep and is
heavy enough to allow the user to "push
off" from it while seated. Its tactile ribbed
surface works well even for users who take
off their shoes.

FootEase™

MANUFACTURER MicroComputer
Accessories
Los Angeles, California

MATERIALS Platinum plastic platform
covered in charcoal gray carpeting.

This adjustable foot rest tilts to any desired angle and locks into position with
just a foot lever. The maximum angle is 23
degrees. When level, the 13 by 19-inch
platform raises feet nearly 4 inches.

213

Palm Rest

DESIGNER   IDTWO and David Kelley
Design

MANUFACTURER   Details, member
Steelcase Design Partnership
New York, New York

MATERIALS   Steel base with nylon upholstered cushion. Neutral colors, chalk and
meteorite, coordinate well with most office
products.

Freestanding and height-adjustable,
Palm Rest accommodates varied keyboard
thicknesses on the market. It works with
keyboards up to 9.5 inches by 22 inches
and fits at the front edge of any work surface. It is specifically designed to provide
static support to help reduce muscle fatigue and strain from computer keying. A
pad cushions the interface surface and is
removable for easy cleaning and
replacement.

Keyboard Platform/Adjustable Wrist Rest

MANUFACTURER   MicroComputer Accessories, A Rubbermaid Company
Los Angeles, California

MATERIALS   Plastic platform with padded
cushion that pops out for cleaning.

The Keyboard Platform, with height-adjustable wrist rest, accommodates keyboards
up to 8½ inches deep and slips underneath the keyboard to adjust its angle. The
padded wrist rest has rotating knobs that
adjust up and down, forward and back, to
accommodate a variety of keyboard depths
and hand sizes. The wrist rest is also available separately.

Articulating Keyboard Support

DESIGNER IDTWO and David Kelley Design

MANUFACTURER Details, member Steel-case Design Partnership
New York, New York

MATERIALS Steel and polycarbonate. Neutral colors, chalk and meteorite, coordinate with most office products.

This fully-adjustable keyboard support provides a supplementary surface which can accommodate a maximum keyboard size of 9.5 by 22 inches. It is vertically height-adjustable from 2 inches above to 12 inches below the work surface and can move 20 inches laterally. The keyboard tray swivels 180 degrees to accommodate shared tasks, and it offers unlimited tilting options. Color-coded tension knobs handle adjustment and locking positions. It raises, lowers, swivels, and tilts for maximum working comfort and to accommodate a wide range of user dimensions and work styles. A height-adjustable palm rest provides wrist support and has a removable padded cover for easy cleaning and replacement. The keyboard attaches to almost any work surface and when stored takes a minimum depth of 20 inches by 27 inches wide, with only a 4-inch infringement into the kneespace. The tray's underside is padded to avoid banged knees and snagged stockings. Optional mouse pad with integral padded mousing surface and unlimited tilt attaches to either side of the keyboard support.

Underdesk Keyboard Drawer

MANUFACTURER MicroComputer Accessories
A Rubbermaid Company
Los Angeles, California

MATERIALS Non-conductive platinum plastic drawer.

The Underdesk Keyboard Drawer is a sliding cantilevered drawer that can be mounted under a work surface to provide adjustability and reduce clutter. It slides on ball-bearings and locks into position. Special mounting brackets allow installation of one of three typing heights. It accommodates keyboards up to 20¼ inches wide, 2¼ to 3¾ inches high, and 10 inches deep. Another model, the Super Underdesk Keyboard Drawer accommodates keyboards up to 22½ inches wide, plus a mouse.

Tilt'n Turn CRT Stand

MANUFACTURER MicroComputer Accessories
A Rubbermaid Company
Los Angeles, California

MATERIALS Platinum-colored, high-impact styrene.

The Tilt'n Turn adjustable stand for PCs and terminals helps users reduce glare, minimize eyestrain, and eliminate neck craning. It fits CRTs with feet separations up to 12 by 12 inches. A built-in tension spring allows full range of adjustment while in use. Tilt'n Turn rotates 360 degrees and supports monitors up to 40 pounds. Anti-skid pads on the top and bottom provide stability.

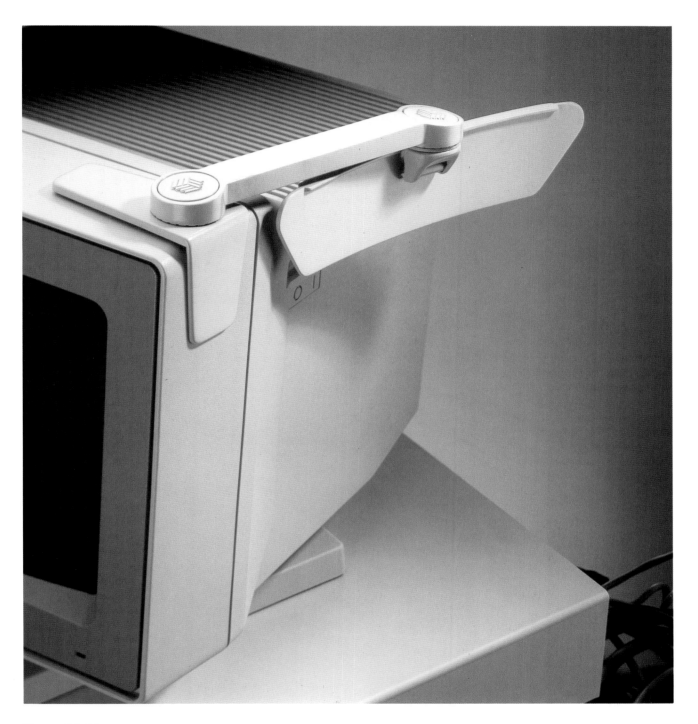

Copy Holder

MANUFACTURER   MicroComputer
Accessories
A Rubbermaid Company
Los Angeles, California

MATERIALS   Platinum-colored high-impact styrene.

Copy Holder reduces eye fatigue by raising copy to monitor level. Its specially designed easel keeps the paper from ruffling in drafts. Arm pivots 180 degrees, and swings out of the way when not in use. Paperholder pivots and can be locked into a preferred position. The San Francisco ordinance requires that document holders with adjustable angle and height be provided upon the request of operators who work at least 4 hours a day.

Ios™

DESIGNER   Stephan Copeland

MANUFACTURER   Details, member
Steelcase Design Partnership
New York, New York

MATERIALS   Polycarbonate arms tinted in
anemone and nile. Each lamp comes with
two shade caps—opaque cap matches color
of arms, and translucent cap comes in jade,
amethyst, and ivory. Charcoal-colored base,
stalk and shade. An all-charcoal version is
available.

The Ios articulated task light has three
pivot points for positioning its head in a
range of 8 to 30 inches from the base. Its
tiltable shade adjusts from 10 to 29 inches
above the work surface. This lamp is ideal
for mounting on any systems furniture
panel, on Steelcase's Context rail, or it can
be used as a freestanding unit with its own
cast iron base. Ios is supplied with a
double-tube fluorescent lamp and is UL-
listed and CSA-approved.

BAP

DESIGNER   Alberto Meda and Paolo
Rizzatto

MANUFACTURER   LUCE PLAN, Distributed
by Artemide
Farmingdale, New York

MATERIALS   Head is molded glass-fiber
with a blue, green or amber filter. Arms are
extruded aluminum. Available in white or
black.

The BAP VDT task lighting system features
three sizes (small, medium, large) and
three models. The head/diffuser with recessed fluorescent lamp on a pantograph-
type arm can be totally rotated and adjusted yet remains parallel to the work
surface. The top of the lamp's head gives
off a cool luminous glow similar to the
computer screen, and has a lamp ejection
button for easy bulb replacement. Available in two arm lengths, 14 inches and 16
inches, with weighted base, surface inserts
or clamps, and floor base.

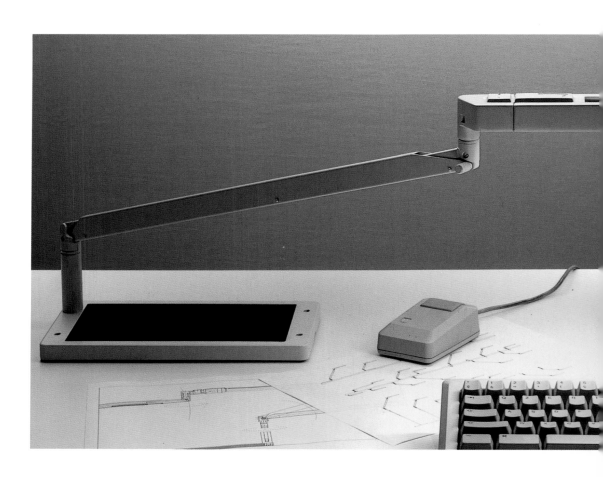

Tango

DESIGNER   Stephan Copeland

MANUFACTURER   Flos Inc.
Huntington Station, New York

MATERIALS   Aluminum body and base available in two colors: anthracite or silver. Head has a urethane diffuser shade. Fluorescent lamp has a plastic shield inside the diffuser and the halogen lamp has an inner metal reflector. Anthracite model has black joints with a green, blue or black shade. Silver version has light gray joints and a green, blue or gray shade.

An adjustable task light with detailed articulating joints, Tango comes equipped with either a halogen or fluorescent lamp. Its pivotal head is held in position by swagged aluminum wireways. The lamp features flexible joints and comes with either a dark gray base or table clamp. A panel mounting bracket is available for use on furniture systems. The fluorescent light source is UL-listed.

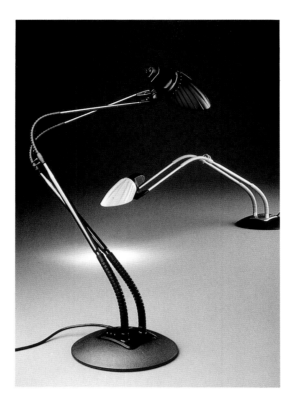

Desk

DESIGNER   Ezio Didone

MANUFACTURER   Flos Inc.
Huntington Station, New York

MATERIALS   Black anodized aluminum body with anodized polished aluminum telescopic arm. Lamp head has an extruded aluminum housing and a ridged acrylic diffuser with an inner polished aluminum reflector.

Desk is an adjustable, fluorescent task light with a telescopic arm, swivel base, two elbow joints, and a 315-degree rotating head. The extruded lens diffuses light from the fluorescent source. Desk is available with a base, table clamp or optional workstation bracket.

Asymmetric Task Lighting

MANUFACTURER   Luxo Lamp Corporation
Port Chester, New York

MATERIALS   Specular reflector system with
ABS plastic housing and stamped steel tube
arms. Monochromatic finish options include non-glare black, white and light gray.

Designed specifically for computer-oriented
workstations or other small work areas,
Asymmetric Task Lighting provides glare-
free light for work surfaces and keyboards
without veiling reflections or washing out
VDT screens. Its duckbill-shaped head,
mounted on an adjustable patented arm,
sports an energy efficient, compact 13-watt
fluorescent lamp. The lamp head's four-part
reflector system allows it to be placed un-
obtrusively outside the line of work. It
is available with clamp, incline-mount,
weighted base, or Luxo's rail-mount system, and it uses in-line, quick-connect
plugs for easy installation in most furniture
systems. Internally mounted springs in the
arms provide parallel motion which maintains the shade in a horizontal position to
the work surface.

Furniture-Integrated Ambient Lighting System

DESIGNER   Peter Ngai & Douglas Herst of
Peerless, Utkan Salman of Harlan Yard,
Tim Stern of Steelcase

MANUFACTURER   Peerless Lighting
Corporation
Berkeley, California

MATERIALS   Die-cast aluminum fixtures.
Fixtures and mountings are available to coordinate with Steelcase custom colors.

This indirect ambient lighting system is
compatible with the VDT-sensitive aesthetic of Steelcase's Avenir, Series 9000,
Elective Elements, and Context furniture
systems. The lights incorporate optical
components, such as a micro-prismatic
specular/diffusing lens, originally found in
the lighting manufacturer's pendant and
wall-mounted fixtures. Mounting options include desk- and cabinet-top, panel edge,
freestanding, and wall/panel, all at above-
standing-eye-level height.

Space Saver System

DESIGNER Sava Cvek

MANUFACTURER Luxo Lamp Corporation
Port Chester, New York

MATERIALS Rail is extruded aluminum in
anodized black and satin aluminum finish.

The Space Saver System is comprised of
lightweight metal rails in standard and custom lengths. It is made up of three main
elements: the Luxo rail mount system and
under-the-counter adaptor; the Luxo
Halogen task lighting system and its Asymmetric collection of task lights; and
copyholders and computer arms. The rail
mount system removes task lighting and
document holders from the work surface
and places them on a wall or furniture
panel, thereby freeing up valuable work
space. The under-the-counter adaptor
mounts lights underneath countertops,
shelves and cabinets. The Space Saver
System also offers three types of mounting
brackets: an individual panel mount, a paper management mount, and an individual
mount with a shaft adaptor which accepts
shaft-mounted products by Luxo and other
manufacturers.

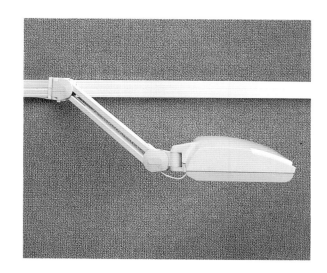

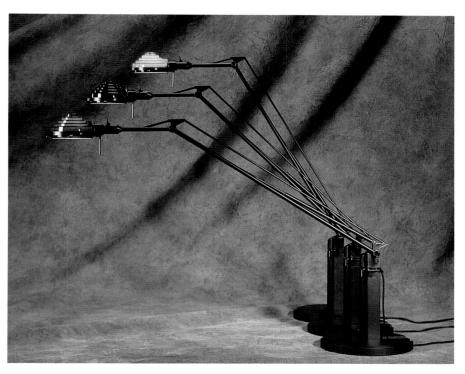

EganCabinets

MANUFACTURER   Egan Visual, Inc.
Ontario, Canada

MATERIALS   Cabinets in four categories:
Wood cabinets in three styles—rectilinear,
bullnose, and traditional—in a variety of
finishes from mahogany to light oak with
optional brass or stainless inlay; Etex cabinets in bullnose and pencil-edge styles with
textured polymer finish in 6 standard or
105 custom colors; Color Contour cabinets
in radius and pencil-edge styles with a
polyurethane coating in 6 standard colors;
Quality Value rectilinear cabinets in wood
veneers or 5 laminate finishes. Tackpanels
are fabric covered. Eganboard writing surface is porcelain on steel.

Visual board cabinets are especially suited
for use in private offices, conference,
meeting, and training rooms. Cabinet doors
open to reveal varied presentation surfaces
including a magnetic porcelain writing surface, a flipchart to hang on either door, two
fabric tackable panels, and a pull-down
projection screen that is standard on all
but QV cabinets. Cabinets are available in
a variety of sizes and finishes, and they
mount flush to the wall. The Copy Cabinet
features Panaboard™ which combines Pan-
asonic copy technology with the Egan
product. It provides a continuous plastic
writing surface with instant copy capabilities. A copy printer scanner on the
bottom of the cabinet scans the writing
surface and produces a copy reduced to an
8½-by-11-inch format. This can enhance
meeting productivity by eliminating the
need for extensive note-taking.

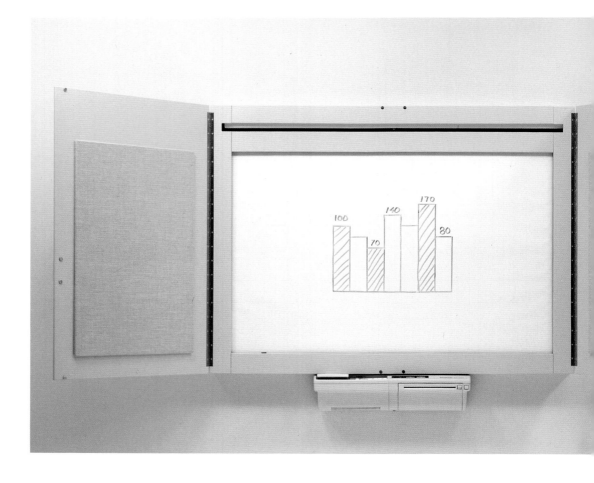

EganSystem

MANUFACTURER Egan Visual, Inc.
Ontario, Canada

MATERIALS Aluminum track with plastic cover. Available in standard taupe and 105 optional Color Plus colors for an upcharge. Epoxy-coated, taupe-colored rigid wire grid display panels. Tackpanels are fabric covered. Etex Cabinetry and shelving units are made with high density fiberboard and finished with the durable polymer Etex finish, in a selection of colors.

EganSystem is a complete range of integrated presentation components that are suspended from unobtrusive tracks on the wall. The Track system is ideal for training and display. Presentation tools on the track include a display shelving unit with wire management for slide projectors. Other features are: friction grips to display flipchart sheets; a reversible tackboard/markerboard; and a grid with adjustable flat or angled shelving and apparel hangers for display or merchandising of three-dimensional objects. There is also a literature display rack for magazines, folders and brochures.

Freestanding items include the Mobile Video Centre with an electric scissor lift that can raise and lower 125 pounds of video equipment. Also available is a Lectern with custom logo.

Mauro Boards and Cabinets

DESIGNER Charles Mauro

MANUFACTURER Hardwood Visuals®
A Howe Company
Trumball, Connecticut

MATERIALS Board and cabinet frames in polished aluminum or 3 powder-coat colors. Porcelain writing surfaces in 3 tones or in black chalkboard. Cabinet face doors available in 14 wood veneers or 7 laminates. Finish option: painted lacquer in choice of 4 colors over walnut wood.

Mauro visual boards and cabinets are known for their clean design, slim profile, and lightweight body. Concealed flip-out trays hold markers and other writing supplies. Mauro Standard Boards function independently or can be linked together to create a continuous writing surface to fit practically any desired length. A unique coupling mechanism attaches to the top and bottom of the boards to align them and keep them together. Mauro Visual Cabinets feature tackboard fabric panels inside each door in 5 colors. Optional accessories include projection screen, markers, erasers, and magnets.

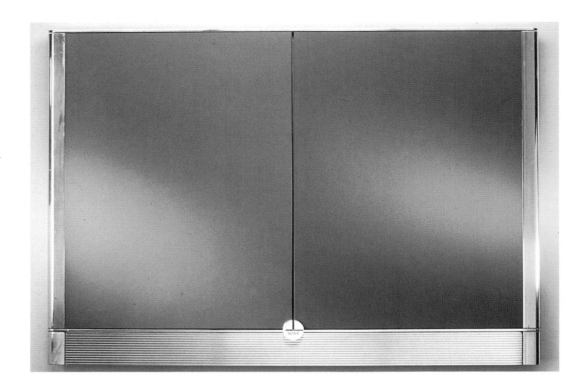

McSort

DESIGNER William Sklaroff

MANUFACTURER McDonald Products, Buffalo, New York

MATERIALS Metal construction with some plastic elements. Available in 13 color choices to coordinate with open plan systems.

The McSort paper management system, designed to mount on furniture system panels, features a broad line of accessories. It is sturdy with good load bearing capabilities. The load bar, available in a selection of lengths, offers end caps and proper mounting brackets. Accessories include a wide variety of load bar-mountable components such as a message and diskette sorter, slanted file sorter, binder bin, correspondence pocket, hanging folder file, plus a range of desk-top items such as a daily calendar, and pencil tray. The utility shelf, in custom lengths, supports books and supplies on top, whereas items such as a tape dispenser, and digital clock mount underneath.

Eldonwal®

MANUFACTURER Eldon Rubbermaid Office Products
Los Angeles, California

MATERIALS Plastic with metal brackets. Available in ebony, smoke, putty, slate blue, gray, and graphite gray.

This paper management system universal bar, with brackets or optional over-the-wall hangers, can easily attach to modular walls and partitions, with or without slotted standards. The bar can also be mounted to permanent walls. It is available in standard 2- to 5-foot lengths or may be cut to specifications. All bars are 3⅝ inches high. Organizing components with built-in back brackets mount securely on the bar. Organizers come in a wide range including division sorters, vertical file boxes, EDP trays, front load trays, and utility shelves.

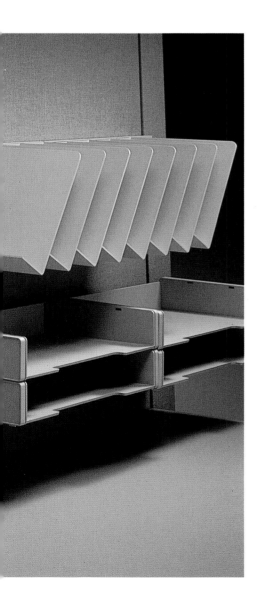

Work Flo

DESIGNER The Richard Penney Group

MANUFACTURER Details, member
Steelcase Design Partnership
New York, New York

MATERIALS Work Flo items may be
specified to coordinate with all Steelcase
paints, laminates, and wood finishes. Plastic parts are available in a variety of colors.

Work Flo is a collection of work tools and
accessories supported on a rail which is
designed to be mounted on any systems
furniture panels. It is meant to improve
work organization and paper flow, free up
work surface space, and provide a more
personal touch. The collection consists of:
a rail system with connectors; supplementary work surfaces for the stacking and
sequencing of projects; storage components for use in overheads, pedestals, and
files; pen and pencil holders; locking storage products for personal items; clothes
hanging accessories, and dry-marker-
board/tackboard/mirror units.

Work Tools

MANUFACTURER Herman Miller
Zeeland, Michigan

MATERIALS Metal rails. Metal tools include arches, shelves, letter trays, etc.
Translucent bins are plastic. Available in
five finishes: black umber, inner tone light,
soft white, medium tone, and slate gray.

Work Tools help make the most of vertical
space by placing papers and other items
within easy reach, reducing work surface
clutter, and organizing the work process.
Work Tools include accessories such as:
cork and fabric tackboards; mini shelves;
horizontal letter trays; arches for holding
papers and books; translucent mini-bins for
paper clips and markers; and hanger pegs.

The tools can be used with Ethospace interiors, the Action Office system, Newhouse
Group and Relay furniture. When projects
or responsibilities change the tools can
also be changed or rearranged, in seconds,
on the panel-mounted rail.

Coat Hooks

MANUFACTURER Eldon Brand Clothing Care
Eldon Rubbermaid Office Products
Los Angeles, California

MATERIALS Molded plastic available in ebony, graphite gray, warm white, and warm gray.

For the open plan office, slotted style or over-the-panel coat hooks help personalize the workplace. The slotted style fits standard and deep set panel slots in single or double hook versions. Holds garments or hangers without slipping because the hook's deep groove prevents unwanted movement. For the enclosed office there is a selection of permanent wall, and on the door or over-the-door style coat hooks. Coordinating hangers, with rounded shoulder angle to help maintain garment shape, can also be specified.

Orchestra

DESIGNER   Bruce Hannah and Ayse Birsel

MANUFACTURER   KnollExtra, The Knoll Group
New York, New York

MATERIALS   Aluminum load bar/info rail with molded plastic components in black, medium gray, burgundy, warm putty, electric blue, white, gray.

This load bar, in 11 standard and special lengths, is designed to fit on panels of any major furniture systems manufacturer. The bracket type should be specified for the specific system. Components are designed to hang or freestand. The scope includes a pencil cup, letter trays, binder bins, tape dispenser, stacking letter trays, calendar, card index, memo tray, vase, business-card holder, disk holder, telephone shelf, utility tray, two-way binder bins, slanted sorter, 3-tier vertical paper pack, file sorter, and clip cup holder. Among the freestanding items are a desk pad and wastebasket. Tack and marker-boards mount on the load bar, wall, panel, or top cap. Fill and task lights mount in panel channels.

Four universal storage drawers, designed by Robert Reuter, can mount under any wood work surface. The line offers locking personal file and keyboard drawers in black steel. The keyboard drawer has a support tray with room for disks in back, and the personal drawer has a channel for pencils with space behind for filing or personal belongings.

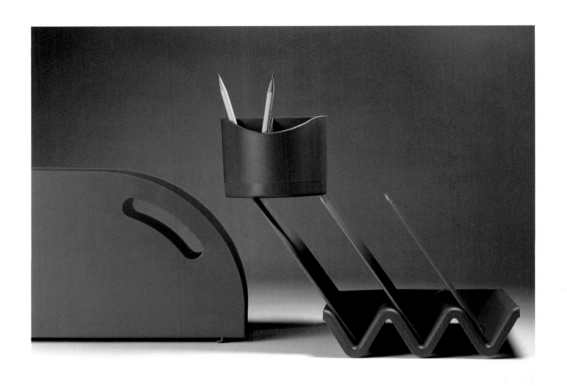

ACKNOWLEDGMENTS

Compiling an informative visual reference book of product resources for the workplace is a task that needs a lot of support systems, and I was fortunate to have many.

The product managers of the firms featured in this book merit particular recognition for patiently answering questions, and for offering information and direction that not only promoted their products but others as well. It was their interest in the outcome of this project that fired my enthusiasm and gave me encouragement. Their assistance and support was indispensable and is greatly appreciated. Here they are:

The Gunlocke Company
Shel Pitney, systems; and Jerome D. Bruckel, seating

Girsberger Industries
Stan Johnson, seating

Haworth, Inc.
Kenneth Malik, seating; Dan Spaans, Portfolio products; Jim Kane, systems; and Jane Nelson, computer support, filing and storage

The Knoll Group
Lou Abbott, Morrison Network; Phil Banas, Equity & ExpanDesk/Tempo; Rick Cranston, Reff System; Brian Harris, filing and storage; David Schutte, accessories; and Scott Starr, seating

Herman Miller, Inc.
Bob Hieftje, seating; Mark Heger, computer support and Ethospace system; Judy Leese, computer support; and Ted Boeve, Action Office

Steelcase, Inc.
Chuck Davis, seating; Frank Doezema, filing and storage; Chuck Halterman, computer support; James Gonda, consultant for competitive assessment group; Edmund Klipa and Peter Jeff, Context system, James Stull, desks and tables; and Mary Underwood, Series 9000

Teknion Office Furniture
Charles Sniffen, Vice President, Product Specialist

Allsteel, Inc.
Barry Swanquist, filing and storage

The participation of the marketing/communication directors and their associates in this project has been most gratifying. Overall, they were remarkably responsive to my requests for more information and better product shots. I am especially thankful to:

Dick Planck of Haworth; Margaret Vaught of Kimball; Coco Kim, Janai Taylor, and Melissa Consovoy of The Knoll Group; Christopher Vogelsang of McDonald Products; Herman Miller's Photographic Librarian, the remarkable Richard Rutledge, for his ready, willing and able assistance; Herman Miller's Communications Department: director, John Berry, along with Dick Holm and Bob Johnston; Peggy Lepp of Office Specialty; James Rutherford of Steelcase; Jacqueline Sargent of Teknion; Brenda Miller Adams of Unifor; Tom Wofford of United Chair; Doris Todd of Vecta Contract; and Elaine Caldwell of Vitra

Public relations/marketing firms that mean business and deliver: Jeff Barnes of Barnes Design Office, Chicago, Illinois, for Johnson Tables; William Kent Schoenfisch of William Kent Schoenfisch Marketing, Rifton, New York, for Meridian and Luxo; Cheryl Hurwitz of Stern + Associates, Cranford, New Jersey, for Steelcase Inc. and Details

The skillful guidance of remarkable Resource Specialists such as Nora Quinn of Total Concept New York Inc.

The following New York architectural design firms for their cooperation and advice:

Juliett Lam of Hellmuth Obata & Kassabaum (HOK); Randolph Gerner of Kohn Pedersen Fox Associates; Jeffrey Simon of SCR; Sidney Philip Gilbert of SPAGA Group; Lou Switzer of The Switzer Group; and Gere Picasso of Engel Picasso Associates in Chatham, New Jersey.

Corporate facility planners:

A special note of thanks to Tina Facos-Casolo of IBM Corporation; Brenda-Lynne Hoffman of the American International Group (AIG); Carol Becker of Merrill Lynch & Co.; and Claudia Lubin of NYNEX Corporation.

My editor:

Susan Kapsis of PBC International for her coaxing, coaching, and editing abilities.

Friends who cheered me on:

Maeve Slavin for her insightful comments and direction
Norman Polsky of Fixtures Furniture for his enthusiastic support and his 800 number
Larry Gardner of Steelcase, Inc. for his input
Networker and people person, Ted Noble, of Furniture Rental Associates
The ultimate enthusiast, Liz Bruder, of Liz Bruder Public Relations;
Kate Flaherty, director A&D Building, who made NEOCON '91 lots of fun

Industry informer, Stephen Viscusi, of The Viscusi Group
Casey MacNamara of Vecta for his suggestions
Lucille Roberts for keeping me in physical shape
Maria Lopez for her help in maintaining my household

To my colleagues on the Steering Committee of Furnish A Future for helping to make it a remarkable success after only one year. Furnish A Future is a program of The Partnership for the Homeless in New York which provides furnishings for relocated homeless individuals and families. Many manufacturers featured in this book have been kind enough to donate furniture and contribute to this worthwhile cause. A special note of praise to the Partnership's Executive Director, Joel Sesser; Furnish A Future Director, Marjory Rice; and its Honorary Chairman, Mrs. Vincent Astor.

Last but not least, to my nearest and dearest:

My husband Conrad Foa, and our sons Justin and Barrett, whose love and support is always there for me;
My parents, Grace and Sam Rimanich, and my brother, Rudy, whom I can always count on

Ultimately my thanks to you, the reader, for supporting my efforts by thinking enough of *Furniture for the Workplace* to purchase it—I hope it works for you.

Appendix 1

FURNITURE SYSTEMS CHRONOLOGY

ALLSTEEL

Panel-based

1979	**8000 Series**
1991	**AURORA**

Desking

1985	**8900 Series**
1992	**Syntrax II**

AMERICAN SEATING

Panel-based

1978	American Seating System
1982	Renamed System R, enhancements
1985	System R changes to accommodate offices and institutions
1988	System R introduces **Invitation Wood** collection
1990	**Framework,** new name for System R
1990	**Framework Clusters** introduced

THE GUNLOCKE COMPANY

Panel-based and Freestanding

1978	Hiebert introduces IPA System
1986	**Prism,** new name for IPA System
1989	**Prism** becomes part of The Gunlocke Company's product line

HAWORTH

Panel-based

1976	**UniGroup,** the first office system with power-integrated panels
1990	**UniGroup Clusters,** an enhancement to the UniGroup open plan system

Panel-based and Freestanding

1988	**PLACES,** a UniGroup update. PLACES goes through three enhancements:
1989	Distinctive Places (a short-lived name) adds enhancements
1989	**Architectural Elements,** varied panel elements work with PLACES and UniGroup
1991	**PLACES/NEW VIEWS,** compatible components for PLACES
1992	**PREMISE,** panel systems to freestanding furniture

Freestanding

1978	**RACE,** a beam and post construction originally introduced by Sunar Hauserman

1990	**RACE** bought and upgraded by Haworth

Desking

KINETICS, *A Haworth Portfolio Company*

1983	**Powerbeam,** a desking system built around a powerbeam
1991	**Powerbeam2,** enhancement gable panels for Powerbeam

THE HON COMPANY

Panel-based

1980	Simplicity introduced
1992	**Simplicity II,** new name for Simplicity
1988	**CONCENSYS,** three office solutions: Systems, Modular, Clusters

KIMBALL OFFICE FURNITURE COMPANY

Panel-based

1988	**Cetra,** known for solid wood elements; now laminates and metal

Panel-based, Freestanding and Track

1992	**Footprint,** provides a bridge between panel systems and casegoods

HARPERS, *a subsidiary of Kimball International*

Panel-based and Freestanding

1984	**Multiple Options**
1992	**Multiple Options,** Kimball acquires Harpers

NATIONAL OFFICE FURNITURE COMPANY, *a subsidiary of Kimball International*

1986	**Officescape** freestanding or connecting fabric-covered panels
1989	**Stepps,** a low-cost, modular collection of furniture

THE KNOLL GROUP

Panel-based and Freestanding System

1986	Morrison System introduced
1990	Morrison System remarketed as **Morrison Network**
1991	**Morrison Network,** enhancements

Panel-based and Freestanding

1982	**Reff System 6,** a premier wood office system
1988	**Reff System Z,** same as Reff System 6 in laminate finishes

Panel-based

1984 WesGroup introduced by Westinghouse Furniture Systems

1990 Equation enhancements, an upgrade to WesGroup

1989/1990 Westinghouse Electric Corp. buys Reff, Shaw Walker, and later, Knoll International. Its Westinghouse Furniture Systems division and its acquisitions are marketed as The Knoll Group.

1991 The Knoll Group markets WesGroup and Equation Systems as WesGroup/Equation

1992 **Equity,** the new name and repackaging of WesGroup/Equation

Panel-based and Freestanding

1977 Shaw Walker System, Tempo 3 panels combined with metal ExpanDesk furniture

1987 Tempo 300 improved performance panels

1992 Shaw Walker System renamed ExpanDesk/Tempo

1992 **ExpanDesk/Tempo** refocused vocabulary and pricing

HERMAN MILLER

Panel-based

1968 **Action Office** system, the world's first panel-based system

1968 **Action Office Series 1** panels for minimal energy and cable management

1986 **Action Office Series 2** panels for increased electrical and cable management

1991 **Action Office Series 3** panels for highest level of panel energy and cable distribution: **A-style** components are the original Action Office components; **B-style** components offer updated features

Frame and Tile

1984 **Ethospace** interiors offers frame-and-tile structured walls

Movable Walls

1982 **V-Wall,** movable, full-height walls

Freestanding Beam-based

1980 **Burdick Group**

Freestanding Furniture

These furniture groups can work on their own, or be integrated with other system environments:

1987 Newhouse Group features table desks that can link and manage cables

1990 Relay, freestanding pieces that move easily and dock together

Remanufacturing Program

1982 **Phoenix Designs,** a Herman Miller subsidiary, solves the problem of furniture disposal with a buy-back and remanufacturing program for Action Office furniture. The product is then offered under the AsNew™ Action Office label.

PANEL CONCEPTS

Panel-based

1976 **System Two.0** basic metal system
System Two.0 cluster units
System Two.0 Shapes, work surface program

1978 **System One.5** bare bones metal panel system

1988 **System Three.0** electrically powered wood system

STEELCASE

Panel-based

1971 Movable Walls, Steelcase's first system

1990 **Avenir,** new name for Movable Walls

Panel-based and Freestanding

1973 **Series 9000** unit assemblies

1978 Series 9000 structural panels

1983 **Valencia,** a wood system for Series 9000

1989 Series 9000 accent panels

1991 Series 9000 enhanced panels

1992 **Valencia Wood Collection** becomes new name for Valencia wood system

Panel-based

1987 **Elective Elements**

Freestanding

1989 **Context,** freestanding workstations with curvilinear work surfaces

Freestanding Desking

1990 **Ellipse,** desk system with horizontal power beam

Work Surface Enhancements

1990 **Tops,** full range of curved tops for panel-mounted applications in all Steelcase systems

Remanufacturing Program

1989 **Revest Inc.** is a subsidiary of Steelcase Inc., headquartered in Tustin, California, with operations in Atlanta, Georgia, and Dallas, Texas. Revest remanufactures furniture for resale or refurbishes furniture for customers who want to have their own products updated. Revest also has a brokerage service through which excess or obsolete furniture is available for purchase from end users.

TEKNION

Panel-based Frame and Tile

1983 **Teknion Office System,** stacking panel modules

Compatible Freestanding Furniture

1988 **Freestanding Laminate Furniture**

1989 **Libretto** wood veneer

Coordinating Storage Line

1990 **Steel Storage** Line

TRENDWAY

Panel-based Systems

1979 **Space Management Systems** (SMS)

1991 **Choices** builds on SMS

Cluster

1987 **TrendCentre,** a cluster workstation approach

Floor-to-Ceiling Partitions

1989 **TrendWall**

UNIFOR, INC.

Freestanding Systems

1986 **Misura ST**

1987 **Mood**

Panels

1989 **Pannelli PL**

Technology Wall

1990 **Progetto 25**

VOKO U.S.

Freestanding Beam-based System

1988 **Univers V-10**

Appendix 2
DIRECTORY

Allsteel Inc.
Allsteel Drive
Aurora, Illinois 60507

American Seating
901 B'way Avenue N.W.
Grand Rapids, Michigan 49504

Artemide Inc.
1980 New Highway
Farmingdale, New York 11735

Atelier International
305 East 63rd Street
New York, New York 10021

The Chair Works
3900 Texas Avenue South, Suite 107
College Station, Texas 77845

Davis Furniture
P.O. Box 2065
High Point, North Carolina 27261-2065

Details
379 West Broadway
New York, New York 10012-4303

Egan Visual
300 Hanlan Road
Woodbridge, Ontario, Canada L4L 3P6

Eldon Rubbermaid Office Products
1130 E. 230th Street
Carson, California 90745-5094

Engel Picasso Associates
21 Warwick Road
Chatham, New Jersey 07928

Fixtures Furniture
1642 Crystal Avenue
Kansas City, Missouri 64126

Flos Inc.
200 McKay Road
Huntington Station, New York 11746

GF Office Furniture
P.O. Box 1108
Youngstown, Ohio 44501

Girsberger Industries
P.O. Box 1476
Smithfield, North Carolina 27577

The Gunlocke Co.
One Gunlocke Drive
Wayland, New York 14572

Karl Guteman
Cornwall
Ontario, Canada

Hardwood Visuals, A Howe Company
P.O. Box 0386
Trumbull, Connecticut 06611-0386

Harpers
2027 Harpers Way
Torrance, California 90501

The Harter Group
Prairie Avenue
Sturgis, Michigan 49091

Haworth Inc.
One Haworth Center
Holland, Michigan 49432-9576

The HON Co.
200 Oak Street
P.O. Box 769
Muscatine, Iowa 52761-0769

Howe Furniture
P.O. Box 0386
Trumbull, Connecticut 06611-0386

ICF Inc.
305 East 63rd Street
New York, New York 10021

Johnson Industries
1424 Davis Road
Elgin, Illinois 60123

Kimball International
1600 Royal Street
Jasper, Indiana 47546

The Knoll Group
655 Madison Avenue
New York, New York 10021

Krueger International
P.O. Box 8100
Green Bay, Wisconsin 54308-8100

Luxo Lamp Corp.
36 Midland Avenue
Port Chester, New York 10573

Mayline Company
619 N. Commerce Street
P.O. Box 728
Sheboygan, Wisconsin 53082-0728

McDonald Products
2685 Walden Avenue
Buffalo, New York 14225

Meridian Inc.
18558 171st Avenue
Spring Lake, Michigan 49456

Metamorphosis Design & Development
430 Tenth Street, Suite N208
Atlanta, Georgia 30318

MicroComputer Accessories
P.O. Box 66911
Los Angeles, California 90066-0911

Herman Miller Inc.
8500 Byron Road
Zeeland, Michigan 49464

Nova Office Furniture
421 West Industrial
Effingham, Illinois 62401

Office Specialty
67 Toll Road
Holland Landing
Ontario, Canada L0G 1H0

Panel Concepts/PCI Tandem
3001 South Tale Street
Santa Ana, California 92704

Peerless Lighting Corp.
2246 Fifth Street
P.O. Box 2556
Berkeley, California 94702-0556

Precision Mfg. Inc.
2200 52nd Avenue
Lachine, Quebec, Canada H8T 2Y6

Sitag U.S.A. Inc.
15131 South Figueroa Street
Gardena, California 90248

Steelcase Inc.
P.O. Box 1967
Grand Rapids, Michigan 49501

Teknion Office Furniture
1150 Flint Road
Downsview, Ontario, Canada M3J 2J5

Thonet International
403 Meacham Road
Statesville, North Carolina 28677

Trendway Corp.
P.O. Box 9016
Holland, Michigan 49422-9016

Unifor Inc.—IDCNY
30-30 Thomson Avenue
Long Island City, New York 11101

United Chair
114 Churchill Avenue N.W.
P.O. Box 96
Leeds, Alabama 35094

Vecta Contract
P.O. Box 534013
Grand Prairie, Texas 75053

Vitra
150 East 58th Street
New York, New York 10155

Voko U.S. Inc.
564 Alpha Drive
Pittsburgh, Pennsylvania 15238

Appendix 3
GLOSSARY

File Systems

FREESTANDING PEDESTALS.   Cabinets with files/box drawers for work surface height applications or used as bases to create desks or credenzas.

LATERAL FILES.   Wide and shallow cabinets with drawers.

VERTICAL FILES.   Narrow and deep cabinets with drawers.

Panels

ACOUSTICAL PANEL.   A sound-reducing, structural panel with a fabric surface.

GLAZED PANEL.   A see-through, structural panel with an acrylic plastic insert.

RACEWAY.   Channels for wire management at the base and/or top of a panel.

TOP CAP.   Trims the top of a panel and can add a quality look when specified in wood veneer.

Storage

CABINETS.   Storage and/or wardrobe cases with hinged, receding or sliding doors.

MOBILE PEDESTALS.   Cabinets with files/box drawers on casters.

OVERHEADS.   Storage units with flipper or recessed doors that are suspended from the top of a furniture system panel.

OVERFILES.   Cabinets that fit on top of lateral files for additional storage.

SUSPENDED PEDESTAL.   A storage unit with drawers that is suspended under panel-hung or freestanding work surfaces.

Work Surfaces

D- b- AND P-SHAPED WORK SURFACES.   Surface configurations are shaped like the letters that describe them, and project out from the panel with a support leg to the floor.

PENINSULA WORK SURFACE.   Round-end or rectangular shaped surface that is supported by the panel/wall and a support leg to the floor. The surface protrudes out from the panel at a 90-degree angle.

TRANSACTION SURFACE.   A surface positioned above a panel to provide counter or display surface.

Appendix 4
CREDITS

Photography courtesy Allsteel **16–19, 132, 138, 187, 204–205;** Photography courtesy American Seating Co. **20–21, 140;** Photography courtesy Artemide **218;** Photography courtesy Atelier International, Ltd. **132, 145;** Photography courtesy Davis Furniture Industries **160, 164–165.** Connect Table Series licensed from Froscher GmbH + CO KG, designed by Manfred Elzenbech; Photography courtesy Egan Visual Inc. **222–223;** Photography courtesy Eldon/Rubbermaid Office Products **210, 225, 227.** Products shown are the proprietary property of Rubbermaid Office Products Group Inc. and all rights with respect to such products are reserved; Disney Installation photos by Marius Rooks **58–59, 119.** Disney Direct Marketing Services, Inc. The Walt Disney Company. Designed by Engel Picasso Associates, Chatham, NJ; Photography courtesy Fixtures Furniture **102–103, 137, 139, 152;** Photography courtesy Flos Incorporated **219;** Photography courtesy GF Office Furniture, Ltd. **137;** Photography courtesy Girsberger Industries, Inc. **98;** Photography courtesy Haworth, Inc. **23–33, 84–85, 76, 110, 139, 158, 162–163, 203;** Photography courtesy Herman Miller, Inc. **6, 45–53, 74, 77, 86–89, 109, 112–113, 124–125, 130, 133, 1148, 155, 202, 206, 226;** Photography courtesy Howe Furniture Corporation **168–169, 174–175, 224;** Photography courtesy ICF Inc. **83, 133, 147, 149;** Photography courtesy Johnson Industries Inc. **178–181;** Photography courtesy Kimball International **12, 36–39, 78, 96–97, 198–199;** Photography courtesy Krueger International **134–135, 142–143, 151, 161, 176–177;** Photography courtesy Luxo Lamp Corporation **220–221;** VariTask™ photography courtesy Mayline Company **112;** Photography courtesy McDonald Products **212, 224;** Photography courtesy Meridian Incorporated **186, 188–193;** Photography courtesy Metamorphosis Design & Development, Inc. **126.** PowerStation® Corner, Power Desk photographed by Charlie Schreiner, Corner PowerStation® photographed by Hedrich Blessing; Photography courtesy Micro-Computer Accessories, Inc., a Rubbermaid Company **213–217;** Photography courtesy Nova Office Furniture, Inc. **109, 122–123;** Photography courtesy Office Specialty-Storwal **200–202;** Photography courtesy Panel Concepts, Inc. **54–44;** Photography courtesy Peerless Lighting Corporation **220;** Photography courtesy Precision Mfg Inc. **108, 116–118;** Photography courtesy Sitag U.S.A. Inc. **104;** Photography courtesy Steelcase Inc. **56–62, 78, 93–95, 111, 120–121, 136, 144, 186–187, 194–195;** Photography courtesy Details, a subsidiary of Steelcase Inc. **210–211, 213–215, 218, 226;** Photography courtesy Teknion Furniture Systems **63–64;** Photography courtesy The Chair Works **99;** Photography courtesy The Gunlocke Company **22, 154, 156;** Photography courtesy The Harter Group **105.** Allegis® is a registered trademark of The Harter Group of Sturgis, MI; Photography courtesy The HON Company **34–35;** Photography courtesy The Knoll Group **40–44, 76, 100–101, 127, 146, 184, 196–197, 211, 228–229;** Photography courtesy Thonet Industries **141;** Photography courtesy Tiffany Office Furniture **128–129;** Photography by Karl Francetic, courtesy Trendway Corporation **65;** Photography by Gabriele Basilico **95–99, 103,** Mario Carrieri **92, 100–101, 182–183,** Francesco Radino **93–94, 102,** courtesy UNIFOR, Inc; Photography © Geoff Knight, courtesy United Chair Company **98;** Photography courtesy VECTA **2, 77, 90–92, 150, 161, 170–173.** Wilkahn FS + Series produced by VECTA under license from Wilkahn GmbH, Germany. U.S. and Canadian patents pending; Photography courtesy Vitra **76, 79–82, 153, 157, 160, 166–167;** Photography courtesy VOKO U.S. Inc. **72–73, 206–207**

INDEX

Products

Designers